STAND OUT

Evidence-Based Learning for College and Career Readiness

2

THIRD EDITION

ROB JENKINS

STACI JOHNSON

NATIONAL GEOGRAPHIC LEARNING

CENGAGE Learning·

Australia • Brazil • Mexico • Singapore • United Kingdom • United States

Stand Out 2: Evidence-Based Learning for College and Career Readiness, Third Edition
Rob Jenkins and Staci Johnson

Publisher: Sherrise Roehr

Executive Editor: Sarah Kenney

Development Editor: Lewis Thompson

Director of Global Marketing: Ian Martin

Executive Marketing Manager: Ben Rivera

Product Marketing Manager: Dalia Bravo

Director of Content and Media Production:
  Michael Burggren

Production Manager: Daisy Sosa

Media Researcher: Leila Hishmeh

Senior Print Buyer: Mary Beth Hennebury

Cover and Interior Designer:
  Brenda Carmichael

Composition: Lumina

Cover Image: Mark Edward Atkinson/Tracey
  Lee/Getty Images

Bottom Images: (Left to Right) Jay B Sauceda/
  Getty Images; Tripod/Getty Images;
  Portra Images/Getty Images; Portra Images/
  Getty Images; Dear Blue/Getty Images; Hero
  Images/Getty Images; Jade/Getty Images;
  Seth Joel/Getty Images; LWA/Larry Williams/
  Getty Images; Dimitri Otis/Getty Images

For product information and technology assistance, contact us at
Cengage Learning Customer & Sales Support, 1-800-354-9706

For permission to use material from this text or product, submit all requests online at **cengage.com**/permissions

Further permissions questions can be emailed to
permissionrequest@cengage.com

Student Book
ISBN 13: 978-1-305-65547-8

National Geographic Learning/Cengage Learning
20 Channel Center Street
Boston, MA 02210
USA

Cengage Learning is a leading provider of customized learning solutions with office locations around the globe, including Singapore, the United Kingdom, Australia, Mexico, Brazil, and Japan. Locate your local office at
www.cengage.com/global

Cengage Learning products are represented in Canada by Nelson Education, Ltd.

Visit National Geographic Learning online at **ngl.Cengage.com**
Visit our corporate website at **www.cengage.com**

Printed in the United States of America
Print Number: 04   Print Year: 2018

ACKNOWLEDGMENTS

Ellen Albano
Mcfatter Technical College, Davie, FL

Esther Anaya-Garcia
Glendale Community College, Glendale, AZ

Carol Bellamy
Prince George's Community College, Largo, MD

Gail Bier
Atlantic Technical College, Coconut Creek, FL

Kathryn Black
Myrtle Beach Family Learning Center, Myrtle Beach, SC

Claudia Brantley
College of Southern Nevada, Las Vegas, NV

Dr. Joan-Yvette Campbell
Lindsey Hopkins Technical College, Miami, FL

Maria Carmen Iglesias
Miami Senior Adult Educational Center, Miami, FL

Lee Chen
Palomar College, San Marcos, CA

Casey Cahill
Atlantic Technical College, Coconut Creek, FL

Maria Dillehay
Burien Job Training and Education Center, Goodwill, Seattle, WA

Irene Fjaerestad
Olympic College, Bremerton, WA

Eleanor Forfang-Brockman
Tarrant County College, Fort Worth, Texas

Jesse Galdamez
San Bernardino Adult School, San Bernardino, CA

Anna Garoz
Lindsey Hopkins Technical Education Center, Miami, FL

Maria Gutierrez
Miami Sunset Adult, Miami, FL

Noel Hernandez
Palm Beach County Public Schools, Palm Beach County, FL

Kathleen Hiscock
Portland Adult Education, Portland, ME

Frantz Jean-Louis
The English Center, Miami, FL

Annette Johnson
Sheridan Technical College, Hollywood, FL

Ginger Karaway
Gateway Technical College, Kenosha, WI

Judy Martin-Hall
Indian River State College, Fort Pierce, FL

Toni Molinaro
Dixie Hollins Adult Education Center, St Petersburg, FL

Tracey Person
Cape Cod Community College, Hyannis, MA

Celina Paula
Miami-Dade County Public Schools, Miami, FL

Veronica Pavon-Baker
Miami Beach Adult, Miami, FL

Ileana Perez
Robert Morgan Technical College, Miami, FL

Neeta Rancourt
Atlantic Technical College, Coconut Creek, FL

Brenda Roland
Joliet Junior College, Joliet, IL

Hidelisa Sampson
Las Vegas Urban League, Las Vegas, NV

Lisa Schick
James Madison University, Harrisonburg, VA

Rob Sheppard
Quincy Asian Resources, Quincy, MA

Sydney Silver
Burien Job Training and Education Center, Goodwill, Seattle, WA

Teresa Tamarit
Miami Senior Adult Educational Center, Miami, FL

Cristina Urena
Atlantic Technical College, Fort Lauderdale, FL

Pamela Jo Wilson
Palm Beach County Public Schools, Palm Beach County, FL

ABOUT THE AUTHORS

Rob Jenkins

I love teaching. I love to see the expressions on my students' faces when the light goes on and their eyes show such sincere joy of learning. I knew the first time I stepped into an ESL classroom that this is where I needed to be and I have never questioned that resolution. I have worked in business, sales, and publishing, and I've found challenge in all, but nothing can compare to the satisfaction of reaching people in such a personal way.

Staci Johnson

Ever since I can remember, I've been fascinated with other cultures and languages. I love to travel and every place I go, the first thing I want to do is meet the people, learn their language, and understand their culture. Becoming an ESL teacher was a perfect way to turn what I love to do into my profession. There's nothing more incredible than the exchange of teaching and learning from one another that goes on in an ESL classroom. And there's nothing more rewarding than helping a student succeed.

Along with the inclusion of National Geographic content, the third edition of **Stand Out** boasts of several innovations. In response to initiatives regarding the development of more complexity with reading and encouraging students to interact more with reading texts, we are proud to introduce new rich reading sections that allow students to discuss topics relevant to a global society. We have also introduced new National Geographic videos that complement the life-skill videos **Stand Out** introduced in the second edition and which are now integrated into the student books. We don't stop there; **Stand Out** has even more activities that require critical and creative thinking that serve to maximize learning and prepare students for the future. The third edition also has online workbooks. **Stand Out** was the first mainstream ESL textbook for adults to introduce a lesson plan format, hundreds of customizable worksheets, and project-based instruction. The third edition expands on these features in its mission to provide rich learning opportunities that can be exploited in different ways. We believe that with the innovative approach that made **Stand Out** a leader from its inception, the many new features, and the new look; programs, teachers, and students will find great success!

Stand Out Mission Statement:

Our goal is to give students challenging opportunities to be successful in their language learning experience so they develop confidence and become independent lifelong learners.

TO THE TEACHER

ABOUT THE SERIES

The **Stand Out** series is designed to facilitate *active* learning within life-skill settings that lead students to career and academic pathways. Each student book and its supplemental components in the six-level series expose students to competency areas most useful and essential for newcomers with careful treatment of level appropriate but challenging materials. Students grow academically by developing essential literacy and critical thinking skills that will help them find personal success in a changing and dynamic world.

THE STAND OUT PHILOSOPHY

Integrated Skills

In each of the five lessons of every unit, skills are introduced as they might be in real language use. They are in context and not separated into different sections of the unit. We believe that for real communication to occur, the classroom should mirror real-life as much as possible.

Objective Driven Activities

Every lesson in **Stand Out** is driven by a performance objective. These objectives have been carefully selected to ensure they are measurable, accessible to students at their particular level, and relevant to students and their lives. Good objectives lead to effective learning. Effective objectives also lead to appropriate self, student, and program assessment which is increasingly required by state and federal mandates.

Lesson Plan Sequencing

Stand Out follows an established sequence of activities that provides students with the tools they need to have in order to practice and apply the skills required in the objective. A pioneer in Adult Education for introducing the Madeline Hunter WIPPEA lesson plan model into textbooks, **Stand Out** continues to provide a clear and easy-to-follow system for presenting and developing English language skills. The WIPPEA model follows six steps:

- **W**arm up and Review
- **I**ntroduction
- **P**resentation
- **P**ractice
- **E**valuation
- **A**pplication

Learning And Acquisition

In **Stand Out**, the recycling of skills is emphasized. Students must learn and practice the same skills multiple times in various contexts to actually acquire them. Practicing a skill one time is rarely sufficient for acquisition and rarely addresses diverse student needs and learning styles.

Critical Thinking

Critical thinking has been defined in various ways and sometimes so broadly that any activity could be classified to meet the criteria. To be clear and to draw attention to the strong critical thinking activities in **Stand Out,** we define these activities as *tasks that require learners to think deeper than the superficial vocabulary and meaning.* Activities such as ranking, making predictions, analyzing, or solving problems, demand that students think beyond the surface. Critical thinking is highlighted throughout so the instructor can be confident that effective learning is going on.

Learner-Centered, Cooperative, and Communicative Activities

Stand Out provides ample opportunities for students to develop interpersonal skills and to practice new vocabulary through graphic organizers and charts like VENN diagrams, graphs, classifying charts, and mind maps. The lesson planners provide learner-centered approaches in every lesson. Students are asked to rank items, make decisions, and negotiate amongst other things.

Dialogues are used to prepare students for these activities in the low levels and fewer dialogues are used at the higher levels where students have already acquired the vocabulary and rudimentary conversation skills.

Activities should provide opportunities for students to speak in near authentic settings so they have confidence to perform outside the classroom. This does not mean that dialogues and other mechanical activities are not used to prepare students for cooperative activities, but these mechanical activities do not foster conversation. They merely provide the first tools students need to go beyond mimicry.

Assessment

Instructors and students should have a clear understanding of what is being taught and what is expected. In **Stand Out**, objectives are clearly stated so that target skills can be effectively assessed throughout.

Formative assessments are essential. Pre and post-assessments can be given for units or sections of the book through *ExamView*—a program that makes developing tests easy and effective. These tests can be created to appear like standardized tests, which are important for funding and to help students prepare.

Finally, *learner logs* allow students to self-assess, document progress, and identify areas that might require additional attention.

SUPPLEMENTAL COMPONENTS

The **Stand Out** series is a comprehensive one-stop for all student needs. There is no need to look any further than the resources offered.

Stand Out Lesson Planners

The lesson planners go beyond merely describing activities in the student book by providing teacher support, ideas, and guidance for the entire class period.

- **Standards correlations** for **CCRS, CASAS,** and **SCANS** are identified for each lesson.
- **Pacing Guides** help with planning by giving instructors suggested durations for each activity and a selection of activities for different class lengths.
- **Teacher Tips** provide point-of-use pedagogical comments and best practices.
- **At-A-Glance Lesson Openers** provide the instructor with everything that will be taught in a particular lesson. Elements include: the agenda, the goal, grammar, pronunciation, academic strategies, critical thinking elements, correlations to standards, and resources.
- **Suggested Activities** go beyond what is shown in the text providing teachers with ideas that will stimulate them to come up with their own.
- **Listening Scripts** are integrated into the unit pages for easy access.

Stand Out Workbook

The workbook in the third edition takes the popular **Stand Out Grammar Challenge** and expands it to include vocabulary building, life-skill development, and grammar practice associated directly with each lesson in the student book.

Stand Out Online Workbook

One of the most important innovations new to the third edition of **Stand Out** is the online workbook. This workbook provides unique activities that are closely related to the student book and gives students opportunities to have access to audio and video.

The online workbook provides opportunities for students to practice and improve digital literacy skills essential for 21st century learners. These skills are essential for standardized computer and online testing. Scores in these tests will improve when students can concentrate on the content and not so much on the technology.

Activity Bank

The Activity Bank is an online feature that provides several hundred multilevel worksheets per level to enhance the already rich materials available through **Stand Out**.

DVD Program

The **Stand Out Lifeskills Video Program** continues to be available with eight episodes per level; however, now the worksheets are part of the student books with additional help in the lesson planners.

New to the third edition of **Stand Out** are two National Geographic videos per level. Each video is accompanied by four pages of instruction and activities with support in the lesson planners.

Examview

ExamView is a program that provides customizable test banks and allows instructors to make lesson, unit, and program tests quickly.

STANDARDS AND CORRELATIONS

Stand Out is the pioneer in establishing a foundation of standards within each unit and through every objective. The standards movement in the United States is as dominant today as it was when **Stand Out** was first published. Schools and programs must be aware of on-going local and federal initiatives and make attempts to meet ever-changing requirements.

In the first edition of **Stand Out**, we identified direct correlations to SCANS, EFF, and CASAS standards. *The Secretaries Commission on Achieving Necessary Skills* or SCANS and *Equipped for the Future* or EFF standards are still important and are identified in every lesson of **Stand Out**. These skills include the basic skills, interpersonal skills, and problem-solving skills necessary to be successful in the workplace, in school, and in the community. **Stand Out** was also developed with a thorough understanding of objectives established by the *Comprehensive Adult Student Assessment Systems* or CASAS. Many programs have experienced great success with their CASAS scores using **Stand Out**, and these objectives continue to be reflected in the third edition.

Today, a new emphasis on critical thinking and complexity has swept the nation. Students are expected to think for themselves more now than ever before. They must also interact with reading texts at a higher level. These new standards and expectations are highly visible in the third edition and include *College and Career Readiness Standards*.

Stand Out offers a complete set of correlations online for all standards to demonstrate how closely we align with state and federal guidelines.

IMPORTANT INNOVATIONS TO THE THIRD EDITION

New Look
Although the third edition of **Stand Out** boasts of the same lesson plan format and task-based activities that made it one of the most popular books in adult education, it now has an updated look with the addition of the National Geographic content which will capture the attention of the instructor and every student.

Critical Thinking
With the advent of new federal and state initiatives, teachers need to be confident that students will use critical thinking skills when learning. This has always been a goal in **Stand Out**, but now those opportunities are highlighted in each lesson.

College And Career Readiness Skills
These skills are also identified by critical thinking strategies and academic-related activities, which are found throughout **Stand Out**. New to the third edition is a special reading section in each unit that challenges students and encourages them to develop reading strategies within a rich National Geographic environment.

Stand Out Workbook
The print workbook is now more extensive and complete with vocabulary, life skills, and grammar activities to round out any program. Many instructors might find these pages ideal for homework, but they of course can be used for additional practice within the classroom.

Media And Online Support
Media and online support includes audio, video, online workbooks, presentation tools, and multi-level worksheets, ExamView, and standards correlations.

CONTENTS

Numeracy/ Academic Skills	CCRS	SCANS	CASAS
• Clarification strategies • Focused listening	RI1, R12, SL2, SL3, L1, L2, L3, RF2, RF3	**Many SCAN skills are incorporated in this unit with an emphasis on:** • Acquiring and evaluating information • Listening • Speaking • Sociability	**1:** 0.1.4, 0.2.1 **2:** 0.1.2, 0.1.4, 0.2.1, 0.2.2, 4.8.1 **3:** 0.1.2, 0.1.5, 0.1.6, 7.5.6
• Making bar graphs • Classifying • Developing study skills • Evaluating • Focused listening • Paragraph writing • Peer-editing • Predicting • Reviewing	RI1, RI2, RI4, RI7, RI10, W2, W4, W8, W9, SL1, SL2, SL4, SL5, L1, L2, L4, L5, RF2, RF3	**Most SCANS are incorporated into this unit with an emphasis on:** • Understanding systems • Seeing things in the mind's eye • Self-management • Sociability (Technology is optional.)	**1:** 0.1.1, 0.1.4, 0.2.1, 7.5.6 **2:** 0.1.2, 0.2.1 **3:** 0.1.2, 1.1.4, 4.8.1, 4.8.6 **4:** 0.1.2, 0.2.1, 0.2.4, 2,3,1, 2.3.2, 7.4.7 **5:** 1.1.5, 2.3.3 **R:** 0.1.1, 0.1.2, 0.1.4, 0.2.1, 0.2.4, 1.1.4, 1.1.5, 2.3.1, 2.3.2, 2.3.3, **TP:** 0.1.1, 0.1.2, 0.1.4, 0.2.1, 0.2.4, 2.3.1, 2.3.2, 2.3.3, 4.8.1
• Classifying • Developing study skills • Evaluating • Focused listening • Peer-editing • Predicting • Reading charts and graphs • Reviewing	RI1, RI2, RI4, RI7, RI9, RI10, W8, SL1, SL2, SL4, SL5, L1, L2, L4, L5, RF2, RF3	**Many SCAN skills are incorporated in this unit with an emphasis on:** • Allocating money • Understanding systems • Arithmetic (Technology is optional.)	**1:** 1.3.9 **2:** 1.1.6, 1.2.1, 1.2.2, 1.2.4, 1.3.9 **3:** 1.1.9, 1.3.9 **4:** 0.1.2, 0.1.3, 1.2.1, 1.2.2, 1.2.4, 1.3.9, 4.8.1 **5:** 0.1.3, 1.3.3, 1.3.9 **R:** 0.1.2, 0.1.3, 1.1.6, 1.1.9, 1.2.1, 1.2.2, 1.2.4, 1.3.3, 1.3.9 **TP:** 0.1.2, 0.1.3, 1.1.6, 1.1.9, 1.2.1, 1.2.2, 1.2.4, 1.3.3, 1.3.9

CONTENTS

Numeracy/ Academic Skills	CCRS	SCANS	CASAS
• Clarifying • Developing study skills • Evaluating • Focused listening • Note taking • Predicting • Reviewing • Scanning • VENN diagrams	RI1, RI2, RI7, RI10, W1, W7, SL1, SL2, SL3, SL4, SL5, L1, L2, L4, L5, RF2, RF3	**Many SCAN skills are incorporated in this unit with an emphasis on:** • Decision making • Problem solving • Self-management (Technology is optional.)	**1:** 1.3.8, 2.6.4 **2:** 1.1.7, 1.3.8 **3:** 1.1.7, 1.3.7, 1.3.8, 2.5.4 **4:** 1.3.8, 3.5.2, 3.5.9 **5:** 1.1.1, 1.1.7, 1.3.8 **R:** 1.1.1, 1.1.7, 1.3.7, 1.3.8, 2.5.4, 2.6.4, 3.5.2, 3.5.9 **TP:** 1.1.1, 1.1.7, 1.3.7, 1.3.8, 2.5.4, 2.6.4, 3.5.2, 3.5.9
• Academic reading • Developing study skills • Evaluating • Focused listening • Negotiating • Note taking • Making pie charts • Predicting • Reviewing • Scanning	RI1, RI2, RI4, RI5, RI7, RI10, SL1, SL2, SL3, SL4, SL5, L1, L2, L3, L4, RF2, RF3	**Many SCAN skills are incorporated in this unit with an emphasis on:** • Allocating money • Arithmetic • Creative thinking • Self-management (Technology is optional.)	**1:** 1.1.3, 1.4.1, 1.4.2, 6.7.2 **2:** 1.4.2 **3:** 1.4.2, 1.4.3 **4:** 4.1.1, 6.1.1, 6.1.3 **5:** 1.5.1, 1.8.1, 6.1.1 **R:** 1.4.1, 1.4.2, 1.4.3, 1.5.1, 6.1.1, 6.1.3 **TP:** 1.4.1, 1.4.2, 1.4.3, 1.5.1, 6.1.1, 6.1.3, 4.8.1
• Brainstorming • Clarification strategies • Classifying • Focused listening • Listening to a lecture • Predicting • Scanning	RI1, RI2, RI7, RI10, W1, W2, W4, W8, W9, SL1, SL2, SL3, SL4, SL5, L1, L2, L4, L5, RF2, RF3	**Many SCAN skills are incorporated in this unit with an emphasis on:** • Acquiring and evaluating information • Writing • Speaking (Technology is optional.)	**1:** 1.1.3, 1.9.4, 2.2.4, 7.2.6 **2:** 2.1.1, 2.4.2 **3:** 1.1.3, 1.9.4, 2.2.1, 2.2.5 **4:** 0.2.3 **5:** 0.2.3 **R:** 0.2.3, 1.1.3, 1.9.4, 2.1.1, 2.2.1, 2.2.5 **TP:** 0.2.3, 1.1.3, 1.9.4, 2.1.1, 2.2.1, 2.2.5, 4.8.1

CONTENTS

Numeracy/ Academic Skills	CCRS	SCANS	CASAS
• Making bar graphs • Developing study skills • Evaluating • Focused listening • Making pie charts • Calculating percentages • Predicting • Reviewing	RI1, RI2, RI4, RI7, RI10, W1, W2, W8, SL1, SL2, SL4, SL5, L1, L2, L3, L4, RF2, RF3	**Many SCAN skills are incorporated in this unit with an emphasis on:** • Understanding systems • Problem solving • Decision making • Self-management (Technology is optional.)	**1:** 3.5.8, 3.5.9 **2:** 3.1.1 **3:** 2.1.8, 3.1.1, 3.1.2, 3.1.3 **4:** 3.3.1, 3.3.2, 3.3.3, 3.4.1 **5:** 2.1.1, 2.1.8, 2.5.1, 3.1.1, 6.7.4 **R:** 3.1.1, 3.1.2, 3.1.3, 3.3.1, 3.3.2, 3.4.1, 3.5.8, 3.5.9 **TP:** 3.1.1, 3.1.2, 3.1.3, 3.3.1, 3.3.2, 3.4.1, 3.5.8, 3.5.9
• Brainstorming • Developing study skills • Evaluating • Focused listening • Reading for main idea • Reviewing	RI1, RI2, RI3, RI4, RI7, RI10, SL1, SL2, SL4, SL5, L1, L2, L3, L4, L5, RF2, RF3	**Many SCAN skills are incorporated in this unit with an emphasis on:** • Organizing and maintaining information • Problem solving • Decision making • Self-management (Technology is optional.)	**1:** 4.4.2, 4.7.3 **2:** 4.1.2, 4.1.8, 4.5.1 **3:** 4.1.1, 4.1.2, 4.1.3, 4.1.6 **4:** 4.1.5, 4.1.7 **5:** 1.7.3, 4.6.1 **R:** 1.7.3, 4.1.1, 4.1.2, 4.1.3, 4.1.5, 4.1.6, 4.1.7, 4.1.8, 4.4.2, 4.5.1, 4.6.1, 4.7.3 **TP:** 1.7.3, 4.1.1, 4.1.2, 4.1.3, 4.1.5, 4.1.6, 4.1.7, 4.1.8, 4.4.2, 4.5.1, 4.6.1, 4.7.3
• Developing study skills • Evaluating • Focused listening • Listening for main idea • Note taking • Paragraph writing • Predicting • Reading a pie chart • Reviewing • Scanning • VENN diagrams	RI1, RI2, RI3, RI4, RI5, RI7, RI10, SL1, SL2, SL3, SL4, SL5, W1, W2, W4, W6, W7, W9, W10, L1, L2, L3, L4, L5, RF2, RF3	**Many SCAN skills are incorporated in this unit with an emphasis on:** • Understanding systems • Knowing how to learn • Responsibility • Self-management (Technology is optional.)	**1:** 4.4.5, 7.1.1, 7.5.1 **2:** 4.4.5, 7.1.1, 7.5.1 **3:** 4.4.5 **4:** 2.5.6, 7.2.7, 7.5.5 **5:** 4.4.5 **R:** 4.4.5, 7.1.1, 7.2.7, 7.5.1, 7.5.5 **TP:** 4.4.5, 7.1.1, 7.2.7, 7.5.1, 7.5.5

Appendices

For other national and state specific standards, please visit: **www.NGL.Cengage.com/SO3**

INTRODUCING
STAND OUT, Third Edition!

Stand Out is a six-level, standards-based ESL series for adult education with a proven track record of successful results. The new edition of *Stand Out* continues to provide students with the foundations and tools needed to achieve success in life, college, and career.

Stand Out now integrates real-world content from National Geographic

UNIT 1

Balancing Your Life

UNIT OUTCOMES
- Analyze and create schedules
- Identify goals and obstacles and suggest solutions
- Write about a personal goal
- Analyze study habits
- Manage time

Look at the photo and answer the questions.
1. What do you think the people are doing?
2. What activities do you do every day?
3. What do you want to do in the future?

Construction workers on beams at the top of the Stratosphere Tower in Las Vegas.

- *Stand Out* now integrates high-interest, real-world content from National Geographic which enhances its proven approach to lesson planning and instruction. A stunning National Geographic image at the beginning of each unit introduces the theme and engages learners in meaningful conversations right from the start.

Stand Out supports college and career readiness

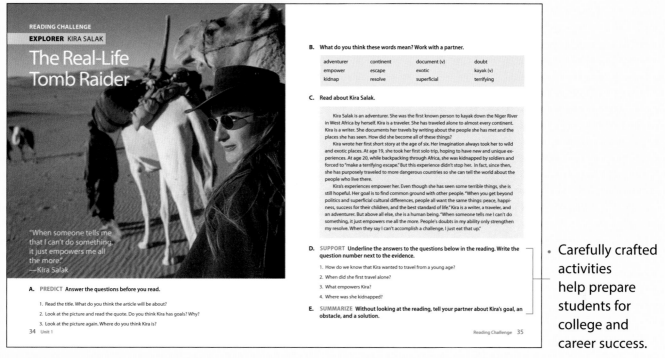

READING CHALLENGE

EXPLORER KIRA SALAK

The Real-Life Tomb Raider

"When someone tells me that I can't do something, it just empowers me all the more."
—Kira Salak

A. PREDICT Answer the questions before you read.

1. Read the title. What do you think the article will be about?

2. Look at the picture and read the quote. Do you think Kira has goals? Why?

3. Look at the picture again. Where do you think Kira is?

34 Unit 1

B. What do you think these words mean? Work with a partner.

adventurer	continent	document (v)	doubt
empower	escape	exotic	kayak (v)
kidnap	resolve	superficial	terrifying

C. Read about Kira Salak.

Kira Salak is an adventurer. She was the first known person to kayak down the Niger River in West Africa by herself. Kira is a traveler. She has traveled alone to almost every continent. Kira is a writer. She documents her travels by writing about the people she has met and the places she has seen. How did she become all of these things?

Kira wrote her first short story at the age of six. Her imagination always took her to wild and exotic places. At age 19, she took her first solo trip, hoping to have new and unique experiences. At age 20, while backpacking through Africa, she was kidnapped by soldiers and forced to "make a terrifying escape." But this experience didn't stop her. In fact, since then, she has purposely traveled to more dangerous countries so she can tell the world about the people who live there.

Kira's experiences empower her. Even though she has seen some terrible things, she is still hopeful. Her goal is to find common ground with other people. "When you get beyond politics and superficial cultural differences, people all want the same things: peace, happiness, success for their children, and the best standard of life." Kira is a writer, a traveler, and an adventurer. But above all else, she is a human being. "When someone tells me I can't do something, it just empowers me all the more. People's doubts in my ability only strengthen my resolve. When they say I can't accomplish a challenge, I just eat that up."

D. SUPPORT Underline the answers to the questions below in the reading. Write the question number next to the evidence.

1. How do we know that Kira wanted to travel from a young age?

2. When did she first travel alone?

3. What empowers Kira?

4. Where was she kidnapped?

E. SUMMARIZE Without looking at the reading, tell your partner about Kira's goal, an obstacle, and a solution.

Reading Challenge 35

- Carefully crafted activities help prepare students for college and career success.

- **NEW Reading Challenge** in every unit features a fascinating story about a **National Geographic explorer** to immerse learners in authentic content.

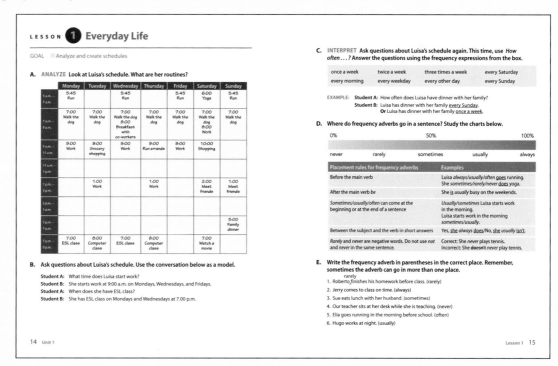

LESSON 1 Everyday Life

GOAL ■ Analyze and create schedules

A. ANALYZE Look at Luisa's schedule. What are her routines?

	Monday	Tuesday	Wednesday	Thursday	Friday	Saturday	Sunday
5 a.m.–7 a.m.	5:45 Run		5:45 Run		5:45 Run	6:00 Yoga	5:45 Run
7 a.m.–9 a.m.	7:00 Walk the dog	7:00 Walk the dog	7:00 Walk the dog 8:00 Breakfast with co-workers	7:00 Walk the dog	7:00 Walk the dog	7:00 Walk the dog 8:00 Work	7:00 Walk the dog
9 a.m.–11 a.m.	9:00 Work	9:00 Grocery shopping	9:00 Work	9:00 Run errands	9:00 Work	10:00 Shopping	
11 a.m.–1 p.m.							
1 p.m.–3 p.m.		1:00 Work		1:00 Work		2:00 Meet friends	1:00 Meet friends
3 p.m.–5 p.m.							
5 p.m.–7 p.m.							5:00 Family dinner
7 p.m.–9 p.m.	7:00 ESL class	8:00 Computer class	7:00 ESL class	8:00 Computer class	7:00 Watch a movie		

B. Ask questions about Luisa's schedule. Use the conversation below as a model.

Student A: What time does Luisa start work?
Student B: She starts work at 9:00 a.m. on Mondays, Wednesdays, and Fridays.
Student A: When does she have ESL class?
Student B: She has ESL class on Mondays and Wednesdays at 7:00 p.m.

14 Unit 1

C. INTERPRET Ask questions about Luisa's schedule again. This time, use *How often . . . ?* Answer the questions using the frequency expressions from the box.

once a week	twice a week	three times a week	every Saturday
every morning	every weekday	every other day	every Sunday

EXAMPLE: **Student A:** How often does Luisa have dinner with her family?
Student B: Luisa has dinner with her family *every Sunday.*
Or Luisa has dinner with her family *once a week.*

D. Where do frequency adverbs go in a sentence? Study the charts below.

0% ————————————— 50% ————————————— 100%

never	rarely	sometimes	usually	always

Placement rules for frequency adverbs	Examples
Before the main verb	Luisa *always/usually/often* <u>goes</u> running. She *sometimes/rarely/never* <u>does</u> yoga.
After the main verb *be*	She <u>is</u> *usually* busy on the weekends.
Sometimes/usually/often can come at the beginning or at the end of a sentence.	*Usually/sometimes* Luisa starts work in the morning. Luisa starts work in the morning *sometimes/usually.*
Between the subject and the verb in short answers	Yes, <u>she</u> *always* <u>does</u>/No, <u>she</u> *usually* <u>isn't</u>.
Rarely and *never* are negative words. Do not use *not* and *never* in the same sentence.	Correct: She *never* plays tennis. Incorrect: She ~~doesn't~~ *never* play tennis.

E. Write the frequency adverb in parentheses in the correct place. Remember, sometimes the adverb can go in more than one place.

rarely
1. Roberto̲finishes his homework before class. (rarely)

2. Jerry comes to class on time. (always)

3. Sue eats lunch with her husband. (sometimes)

4. Our teacher sits at her desk while she is teaching. (never)

5. Elia goes running in the morning before school. (often)

6. Hugo works at night. (usually)

Lesson 1 15

- **EXPANDED Critical Thinking Activities** challenge learners to evaluate, analyze, and synthesize information to prepare them for the workplace and academic life.

- **NEW Video Challenge** showcases **National Geographic footage and explorers**, providing learners with the opportunity to synthesize what they have learned in prior units through the use of authentic content.

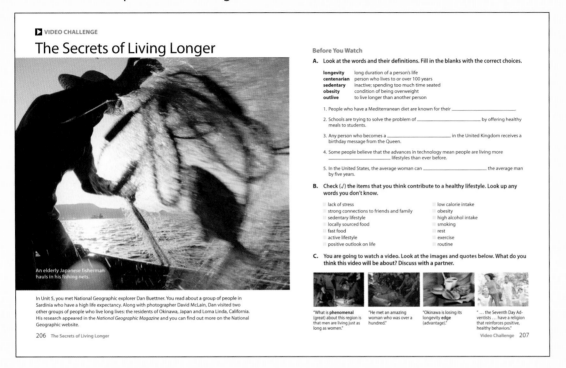

▶ VIDEO CHALLENGE

The Secrets of Living Longer

An elderly Japanese fisherman hauls in his fishing nets.

In Unit 5, you met National Geographic explorer Dan Buettner. You read about a group of people in Sardinia who have a high life expectancy. Along with photographer David McLain, Dan visited two other groups of people who live long lives: the residents of Okinawa, Japan and Loma Linda, California. His research appeared in the *National Geographic Magazine* and you can find out more on the National Geographic website.

206   The Secrets of Living Longer

Before You Watch

A. Look at the words and their definitions. Fill in the blanks with the correct choices.

longevity	long duration of a person's life
centenarian	person who lives to or over 100 years
sedentary	inactive; spending too much time seated
obesity	condition of being overweight
outlive	to live longer than another person

1. People who have a Mediterranean diet are known for their _____

2. Schools are trying to solve the problem of _____ by offering healthy meals to students.

3. Any person who becomes a _____ in the United Kingdom receives a birthday message from the Queen.

4. Some people believe that the advances in technology mean people are living more _____ lifestyles than ever before.

5. In the United States, the average woman can _____ the average man by five years.

B. Check (✓) the items that you think contribute to a healthy lifestyle. Look up any words you don't know.

- lack of stress
- strong connections to friends and family
- sedentary lifestyle
- locally sourced food
- fast food
- active lifestyle
- positive outlook on life
- low calorie intake
- obesity
- high alcohol intake
- smoking
- rest
- exercise
- routine

C. You are going to watch a video. Look at the images and quotes below. What do you think this video will be about? Discuss with a partner.

"What is **phenomenal** (great) about this region is that men are living just as long as women."

"He met an amazing woman who was over a hundred."

"Okinawa is losing its longevity **edge** (advantage)."

"… the Seventh Day Adventists … have a religion that reinforces positive, healthy behaviors."

Video Challenge   207

LIFESKILLS ▶ **My Schedule is Crazy**

Before You Watch

A. Look at the picture and answer the questions.

1. What's wrong with Hector?
2. What do you think Naomi is saying to Hector?

While You Watch

B. ▶ Watch the video and complete the dialog.

Naomi: … you wouldn't skip a day of work, either. Treat your studies in the same way, and your grades will (1) __improve__

Hector: That's a great (2) _____, thanks.

Naomi: Well, now you know what you have to do. So go do it! If you get (3) _____, you'll feel more productive. Trust me!

Hector: (4) _____ give it a try. What have I got to lose, right?

Naomi: Good luck. Tell me how it's (5) _____ later on.

Hector: I (6) _____. Talk to you later.

Check Your Understanding

C. Circle the correct word to complete each sentence.

1. There's too much noise and it's difficult for Hector to (communicate/concentrate).
2. Hector says his (schedule/organization) is crazy and he has no time to study.
3. Naomi suggests that Hector (make time/write down) where and when he going to study.
4. A schedule will help Hector to (get organized/spend time with friends).
5. Naomi tells Hector a schedule will make him (productive/smarter).

Lifeskills Video   29

- The **Lifeskills Video** is a dramatic video series integrated into each unit of the student book that helps students learn natural spoken English and apply it to their everyday activities.

Pages shown are from *Stand Out*, Third Edition Level 3

- **NEW Online Workbook** engages students and supports the classroom by providing a wide variety of auto-graded interactive activities, an audio program, video from National Geographic, and pronunciation activities.

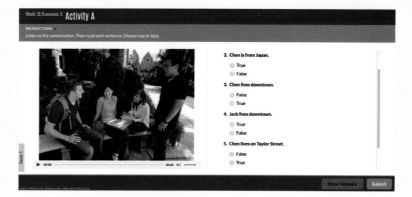

- **UPDATED Lesson Planner** includes correlations to **College and Career Readiness Standards (CCRS), CASAS, SCANS** and reference to **EL Civics** competencies to help instructors achieve the required standards.

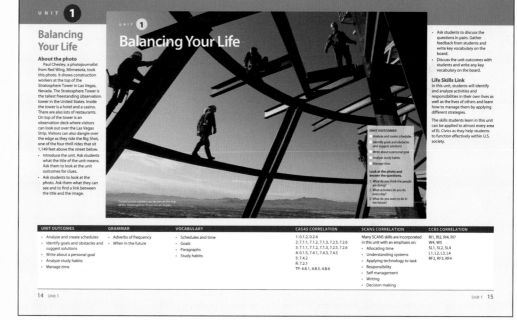

- **Teacher support** *Stand Out* continues to provide a wide variety of user-friendly tools and interactive activities that help teachers prepare students for success while keeping them engaged and motivated.

Stand Out supports teachers and learners

LEARNER COMPONENTS
- Student Book
- Online workbook powered by My**ELT**
- Print workbook

TEACHER COMPONENTS
- Lesson Planner
- Classroom DVD
- Assessment CD-ROM
- Teacher's companion site with Multi-Level Worksheets

Welcome

UNIT OUTCOMES

- Greet people and describe feelings
- Complete a registration form
- Follow instructions

LESSON 1 Nice to meet you!

GOAL ▮ Greet people and describe feelings

A. PREDICT Look at the picture. Where are the students? Who is the new student?

B. Listen and practice.

CD 1
TR 1

Mario:	Hello, what's your name?
Lien:	My name is Lien.
Mario:	Nice to meet you, Lien. I'm Mario.
Lien:	Hi, Mario. Nice to meet you, too.
Mario:	Welcome to our class, Lien.

C. Listen to the conversations. Circle the new student.

CD 1
TR 2-5

1. Mario   (Lien)

2. Esteban   Cecilia

3. Alexi   Jonathan

4. Rick   Nadia

D. **Look at the pictures of feelings. Say the words.**

nervous

sad

tired

happy

angry

hungry

E. **Listen and repeat.**

/m/

I'm nervous.

I'm sad.

I'm tired.

I'm happy.

F. **Practice the conversations.**

Mario:	Hi, Lien!
Lien:	Hello, Mario.
Mario:	How are you today?
Lien:	I'm <u>nervous</u>.
Mario:	Me, too.

Jonathan:	Hi, Alexi!
Alexi:	Hello, Jonathan.
Jonathan:	How are you today?
Alexi:	I'm <u>sad</u>.
Jonathan:	Not me. I'm <u>happy</u> today.

G. **Practice the conversations in Exercise F with a partner. Use different feelings.**

H. Study the chart with your classmates and teacher.

The Verb *Be*			
Subject	***Be***	**Feelings**	**Example sentence**
I	am	fine	I **am** fine. (I'**m** fine.)
You, We, They	are	nervous	You **are** nervous. (You'**re** nervous.)
		sad	We **are** sad. (We'**re** sad.)
		tired	They **are** tired. (They'**re** tired.)
He, She, It	is	angry	He **is** angry. (He'**s** angry.)
		hungry	She **is** hungry. (She'**s** hungry.)

I. Complete the sentences with the correct form of the verb *Be*.

1. Mauricio _____is_____ tired today.

2. They _____are_____ hungry.

3. Antonio and I _____am_____ angry.

4. I _____am_____ fine, thank you.

5. Alice _____is_____ nervous.

6. You _____are_____ happy.

J. **SURVEY** Ask classmates. Write their answers in the table.

Student name	Feelings (How are you today?)
Mario	happy
DOUGLAS	

K. In a group, talk about your conversations.

EXAMPLE: Mario's happy.

LESSON ② What's your name and number?

GOAL ▮ Complete a registration form

A. INTERPRET Read Mario's school registration form.

B. Write the information.

1. Mario's last name is *Garcia* .

2. His phone number is *714 555 7564* .

3. His address is *8237 Henderson Lane* .

4. His zip code is _____ .

5. His date of birth is _____ .

C. Listen and write the information you hear.

CD 1
TR 7

1. My first name is _____ .

2. My last name is _____ .

3. I live on _____ . (street address)

4. I live in *Sou Salito* . (city)

5. I am from _____ .

6. My teacher's last name is *Mis Parelli* .

D. Listen and practice saying the numbers.

0	1	2	3	4	5	6	7	8	9
10	11	12	13	14	15	16	17	18	19
20	21	22	23	24	25	26	27	28	29
30	40	50	60	70	80	90	100		

E. Listen and write the phone numbers you hear.

1. (619) 555-6391   2. 631 555 5100   3. 685 555 28

4. 915 555   5. 33 555 3067   6. 347 555 1743

F. Listen to the conversations. Write the missing information.

1. My name is Marie. I live in Palm City. I go to West Palm Adult School. My phone number is 555 4369.
My last name is Collell.

2. My name is Kenji. I'm from Japan. My address is 6789 Third Street.

3. My name is Mario. It's nice to meet you. My phone number is 555 7899. My address is 37 Hamilton Street.

G. Study the chart with your classmates and teacher.

Possessive Adjectives		
Pronoun	**Possessive adjective**	**Example sentence**
I	My	**My** address is 3356 Archer Boulevard.
You	Your	**Your** phone number is 555-5678.
He	His	**His** last name is Jones.
She	Her	**Her** first name is Lien.
We	Our	**Our** teacher is Mr. Kelley.
They	Their	**Their** home is in Sausalito.

H. Write the possessive adjective.

1. I live in San Francisco. _My_ address is 2354 Yerba Buena.

2. They live in Portland. _Their_ phone number is 555-6732.

3. We live in Dallas. _Our_ last name is Peters.

4. Maria is a happy woman. _____ school is in New York.

5. He is a good student. _____ name is Esteban Garcia.

6. You live on Hilton Street. _____ home is in Rockledge. Is that right?

I. APPLY Talk to a partner. Complete the form with your partner's information.

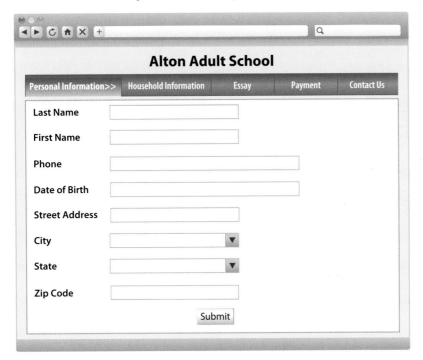

GOAL Follow instructions

A. **Match the instructions with the pictures. Write the correct letter next to each sentence.**

a.

b.

c.

d.

_c_ 1. Listen to the recording.

_b_ 2. Open the book.

_d_ 3. Talk to a partner.

_a_ 4. Go to the board.

B. **Work with a partner. Circle the words that describe classroom activities.**

(answer)   ride   (take out)

eat   run   (talk)

(listen)   (sit down)   (watch)

(open)   sleep   (work)

(practice)   (stand up)   (write)

C. **PREDICT** Look at the picture. What's wrong with Kenji?

🎧 **D.** **Read and listen to the conversation.**

CD 1
TR 13

Mr. Jones:	Kenji, please write a sentence on the board.
Kenji:	Excuse me?
Mr. Jones:	Write a sentence on the board.
Kenji:	I'm sorry, I don't understand.
Mr. Jones:	I can help you. Please come to the board.
Kenji:	OK.

E. **Study the clarification phrases with your classmates and teacher.**

I'm sorry, I don't understand.	Excuse me?
Please speak slower.	Can you say that again, please?
Please speak louder.	Can you spell that?

🎧 **F.** **Listen and circle a clarification phrase. There can be more than one answer.**

CD 1
TR 14

1. Please speak slower.	Can you spell that?	Excuse me?
2. I'm sorry, I don't understand.	Can you say that again?	Can you spell that?
3. Please speak louder.	Please speak slower.	Can you say that again?
4. I'm sorry, I don't understand.	Please speak slower.	Excuse me?

G. Study the chart with your classmates and teacher.

Questions with *Can*			
Can	Pronoun	Verb	Example sentence
Can	you	help	Can you help me?
		answer	Can you answer the question?
		repeat	Can you repeat that, please?
		say	Can you say it again, please?
		speak	Can you speak slower?
		spell	Can you spell it, please?

YES/NO QUESTIONS

Yes/No questions have rising intonation.

Can you help me?

Can you speak slower?

H. **CLARIFY** Complete the conversation with questions from the chart above. Then, practice the conversation with a partner.

Student A: I have a problem. _Can you help me?_____

Student B: Sure.

Student A: Your name is difficult to write. _____

Student B: Yes, it is R-O-X-A-N-N-A.

Student A: You speak very fast. _____

Student B: Yes, of course. It's R-O-X-A-N-N-A.

Student A: Thanks!

CD 1
TR 15

I. Listen and write the instructions.

1. _____

   _____

2. _____

   _____

3. _____

   _____

4. _____

   _____

5. _____

   _____

6. _____

   _____

Everyday Life

A woman gets ready to board a subway train.

UNIT OUTCOMES

☐ Ask for and give personal information

☐ Identify family relationships

☐ Describe people

☐ Interpret and write schedules

☐ Interpret information about weather

Look at the photo and answer the questions.

1. What does the woman look like?

2. Where do you think she is going?

LESSON 1 Where are you from?

GOAL ■ Ask for and give personal information

A. Look at the map. Draw a line from your country to where you live now.

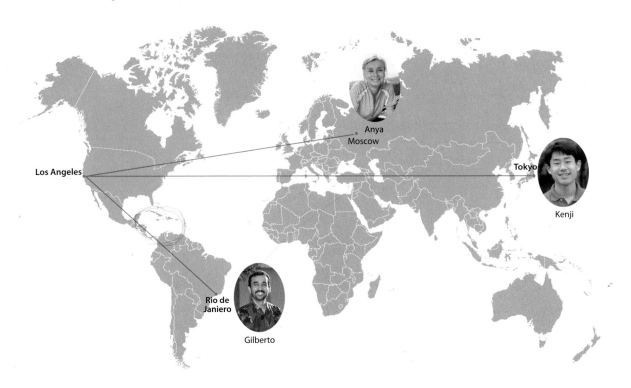

B. Write

1. Kenji is from _TOKYO JOPON_.

   He lives in _Los angeles califarnie_.

2. Anya is from _Moscow Russia_.

   She lives in _Los angeles califarnie_.

3. Gilberto is from _Brazil Rio de Janeiro_.

   He lives in _Los Ageles califarnie_.

4. I am from _Dominican Republica_.

   I live in _Freeport N.Y_.

5. My partner is from _guallaguil escuador_.

   He/She lives in _Freeport_.

14   Unit 1

C. **CLASSIFY** Read the words in the box and complete the table.

25 years old	divorced	single
city	married	state
~~country~~	old	young

Marital status	Age	Place
divorced		*country*

 **D.** Listen to the conversation. Then, use the information about the students to make new conversations.

CD 1
TR 16

Kenji	**Anya**	**Gilberto**	**Marie**
Single	Married	Single	Divorced
22 years old	68 years old	30 years old	32 years old
Tokyo, Japan	Moscow, Russia	Rio de Janeiro, Brazil	Port-au-Prince, Haiti

Gilberto: Where is Kenji from?
Marie: He's from Japan.
Gilberto: How old is he?
Marie: He's 22 years old.
Gilberto: Is he married?
Marie: No, he's single.

QUESTION INTONATION

Yes/No questions have rising intonation.

Is he married?

Information questions have falling intonation.

Where is Kenji from?

E. **Study the charts with your classmates and teacher.**

Simple Present: *Live*			
Subject	**Verb**	**Information**	**Example sentence**
I, We, You, They	live	in Los Angeles in California in the United States	I **live** in Los Angeles. You **live** in Los Angeles, California.
He, She	lives		He **lives** in the United States. She **lives** in Mexico.

Simple Present: *Be*			
Subject	**Verb**	**Information**	**Example sentence**
I	am	from Mexico	I **am** from Mexico.
We, You, They	are	single divorced	We **are** single. You **are** 23 years old.
He, She	is	23 years old	He **is** divorced. She **is** from Vietnam.

🎧 **F.** **Listen to the information about Mario and Lien. Complete the sentences.**

CD 1
TR 17

1. Lien _____*is*_____ from Ho Chi Minh City, Vietnam.

2. She _____*is*_____ 28 years old.

3. She _____*lives*_____ in _____.

4. Mario is ____*lives*____ years old.

5. He also ____*lives*____ in Los Angeles.

6. He _____ from _____.

7. Mario and Lien are not married. They _____.

G. **SURVEY** Ask classmates for personal information and write sentences. Then, share the information with the class.

_____

_____

_____

LESSON 2 Kenji's family

GOAL ▪ Identify family relationships

🎧 **A.** **INTERPRET** Read and listen to Kenji's story. How many people are in his family?

CD 1
TR 18

> My name is Kenji Nakamura. I have a wonderful family. We live in the United States. I have one sister and two brothers. I also have uncles and an aunt here. My father has two brothers and no sisters. My mother has one brother and one sister. My grandparents are in Japan. I'm sad because they are not here with my family.

B. Read Kenji's story again and complete the sentences.

1. Kenji has _onesister_ sister.

2. Kenji has _two brothers_ brothers.

3. Kenji's father has _____ brothers and _____ sisters.

4. Kenji's mother has _____ sister and _____ brother.

C. Look at Kenji's family tree.

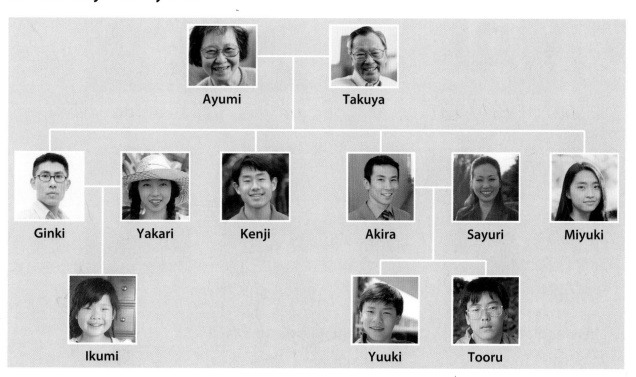

Ayumi — Takuya

Ginki   Yakari   Kenji   Akira   Sayuri   Miyuki

Ikumi   Yuuki   Tooru

D. Study the words with your classmates and teacher.

parents	daughter	aunt	grandfather
father	son	uncle	grandmother
mother	brother	niece	grandson
husband	sister	nephew	granddaughter
wife	cousin		

E. Look at the family tree in Exercise C. Write the correct words under each picture.

1. grandfather / granddaughter

2. husband / wife

3. mother / daughter

4. grandmoth / grandson

5. aunt / niece

6. _____ / _____

F. Ask and answer questions about the people in Exercise E.

EXAMPLE: **Student A:**   How are Takuya and Ikumi related?
   Student B: They are grandfather and granddaughter.

G. **Study the chart with your classmates and teacher.**

Present Simple: *Have*			
Subject	**Verb**	**Information**	**Example sentence**
I, You, We, They	have	three brothers two sisters	I **have** three brothers. You **have** two sisters.
He, She	has	no cousins three sons	He **has** no cousins. She **has** three sons.

H. **Listen. Circle the correct form of *have* and write the missing information.**

CD 1
TR 19

1. Thanh have/(has) _3_ sisters.

2. (I) have/has _3_ brothers.

3. Ricardo and Patty (have)/has _3_ children.

4. Orlando, you (have)/has _3 8_ cousins.

5. Maria have/(has) _2_ sisters.

6. We (have)/has _____ child.

I. **APPLY** On a separate piece of paper, make a bar graph like the one below. Talk to four classmates.

You: How many brothers and sisters do you have?

Juan: I have three brothers and two sisters.

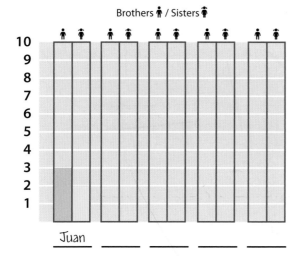

J. **CREATE** Design your own family tree and share it with the class.

LESSON **3** Kenji's class

GOAL ▮ Describe people

A. **Look at the picture of Kenji's class. Who is tall? Who has blond hair?**

Height: short, average height, tall	**Eyes:** brown, blue, green, gray, hazel
Weight: thin, average weight, heavy	**Hair:** black, brown, blond, red, gray, white
He **is** tall and average weight.	She **has** brown eyes and black hair.

B. **Describe four of the students in Exercise A. Use the words from the boxes.**

1. Dalva has green eyes and blond hair.
2. Sung has Black Hair and Black eyes
3. Gilberto has brown and brown ayes
4. Marien has Black eyes and Black hair

C. Listen and complete the bar graph about Kenji's class. Write sentences.

CD 1
TR 20

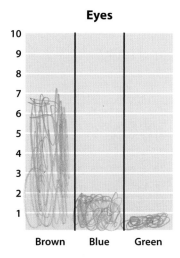

Eyes

1. _Seven students have brown eyes._

2. _____

3. _____

D. **ANALYZE** Look at the picture in Exercise A. In a group, fill in the bar graphs about Kenji's class.

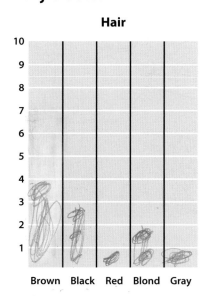

Hair

Brown   Black   Red   Blond   Gray

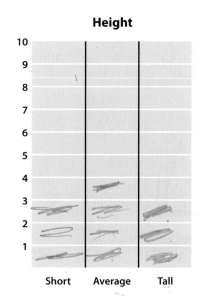

Height

Short   Average   Tall

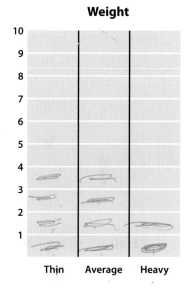

Weight

Thin   Average   Heavy

E. Practice the conversation. Then, look at the picture in Exercise A and describe a student from Kenji's class. Your partner will guess who it is.

Student A: He is short and has black hair. Guess who.

Student B: Mario?

Student A: Yes, that's right. / No, try again.

F. **Read the chart with your classmates and teacher.**

Comparative and Superlative Adjectives		
Adjective	Comparative adjective	Superlative adjective
tall	taller	the tallest
short	shorter	the shortest
old	older	the oldest
young	younger	the youngest

> **THAN**
>
> Use *than* when using comparative adjectives. Henry is taller *than* Karen.

G. **COMPARE** **In a group, answer the questions about Kenji's class.**

1. Who is taller than Kenji? _Lien is taller than Kenji._

2. Who is the tallest in the class? _____

3. Who is shorter than Dalva? _____

4. Who is the shortest in the class? _____

5. Who is the youngest in the class? _____

6. Who is older than the teacher? _____

H. **INTERPRET** **Read the paragraph.**

> There are thirty students in my class. Twenty-five students have black hair. Five students have brown hair. The tallest student in the class is Francisco. The shortest is Eva. I think the youngest student is Nadia.

I. **APPLY** **Write a paragraph about your class. Use the paragraph in Exercise H as a model.**

_____

_____

_____

_____

_____

_____

LESSON **4** My schedule

GOAL ▪ Interpret and write schedules

A. PREDICT Look at the picture. Who is the old woman talking to? Where is she?

B. Read and listen to the conversation.

CD 1
TR 21

Grandmother:	What time is it there?
Larissa:	It's four o'clock.
Grandmother:	What do you do at four o'clock?
Larissa:	I go to school.

C. INTERPRET Practice the conversation. Use the information in the schedule to make new conversations.

Grandmother:	What do you do at <u>four o'clock</u>?
Larissa:	I <u>go to school.</u>

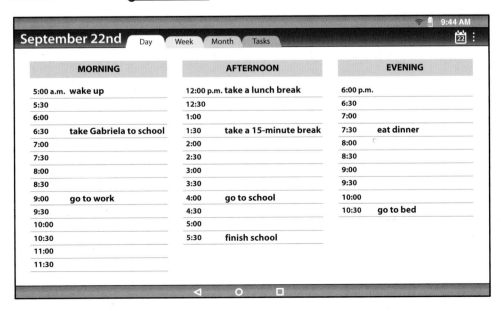

September 22nd — Day / Week / Month / Tasks — 9:44 AM

MORNING	AFTERNOON	EVENING
5:00 a.m. wake up	12:00 p.m. take a lunch break	6:00 p.m.
5:30	12:30	6:30
6:00	1:00	7:00
6:30 take Gabriela to school	1:30 take a 15-minute break	7:30 eat dinner
7:00	2:00	8:00
7:30	2:30	8:30
8:00	3:00	9:00
8:30	3:30	9:30
9:00 go to work	4:00 go to school	10:00
9:30	4:30	10:30 go to bed
10:00	5:00	
10:30	5:30 finish school	
11:00		
11:30		

D. **INTERPRET** Read the information on Gilberto's calendar. Then, listen and point to the days.

CD 1
TR 22

Calendar ∨	⊕ **New** ∨	**Import** **Share** ∨				🙂 ⚙

Gilberto's Calendar

SUNDAY	MONDAY	TUESDAY	WEDNESDAY	THURSDAY	FRIDAY	SATURDAY
		1 wake up at 5:00 a.m. go to school work	**2** wake up at 5:00 a.m. go to school help with children work	**3** wake up at 5:00 a.m. go to school work	**4** wake up at 5:00 a.m. go to school work	**5** wake up at 5:00 a.m. work overtime
6 wake up at 6:00 a.m. play soccer	**7** wake up at 5:00 a.m. go to school help with children work	**8** wake up at 5:00 a.m. go to school work	**9** wake up at 5:00 a.m. go to school help with children work	**10** wake up at 5:00 a.m. go to school work	**11** wake up at 5:00 a.m. go to school work	**12** wake up at 5:00 a.m. take bus to the beach
13 wake up at 6:00 a.m. play soccer	**14** wake up at 5:00 a.m. go to school help with children work	**15** wake up at 5:00 a.m. go to school work	**16** wake up at 5:00 a.m. go to school help with children work	**17** wake up at 5:00 a.m. go to school work	**18** wake up at 5:00 a.m. go to school work	**19** wake up at 5:00 a.m. work overtime

E. Circle the answers to the questions about the calendar.

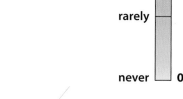

1. What does Gilberto do from Monday to Friday?

   a. He goes to the beach.

   b. He works and goes to school.

   c. He plays soccer.

2. What does he do every Monday and Wednesday?

   a. He helps with the children.

   b. He works overtime.

   c. He wakes up at 7:00 a.m.

F. Circle *True* or *False* for each sentence.

1. Gilberto sometimes goes to work on Saturday.   True   False

2. He never plays soccer on Sunday.   True   False

3. He always gets up at 5:00 a.m.   True   False

4. He often helps with the children.   True   False

G. Study the chart with your classmates and teacher.

Simple Present			
Subject	**Verb**	**Information**	**Example sentence**
I, You, We, They	eat go help play	lunch to school with the children soccer	I **eat** lunch at twelve o'clock. You **go** to school at 8:00 a.m. We sometimes **help** with the children. They **play** soccer on Saturday.
He, She	eat**s*** goe**s**** help**s*** play**s****	lunch to school with the children soccer	He **eats** lunch at twelve o'clock. Nadia **goes** to school at 10:00 a.m. Gilberto **helps** with the children. She **plays** soccer on Friday.
Pronunciation: */s/ **/z/			

H. Practice the conversation. Use Gilberto's calendar in Exercise D to make new conversations.

Student A: What does Gilberto do on Monday?
Student B: He works and goes to school on Monday.

I. APPLY Work with a partner. Ask: "What do you do in the morning?" Write your partner's schedule for the morning. Then, report to a group.

GOAL ▮ Interpret information about weather

A. Review the words and icons with your teacher.

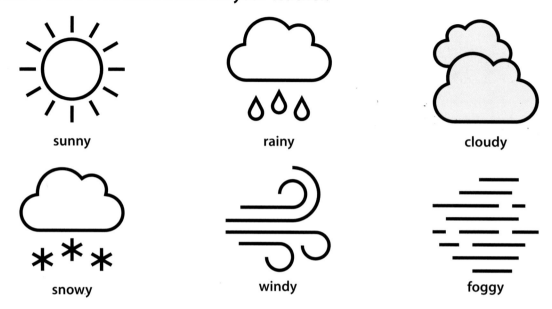

sunny

rainy

cloudy

snowy

windy

foggy

🎧 B. Listen to the weather report and write the correct temperatures on the map.

CD 1
TR 23

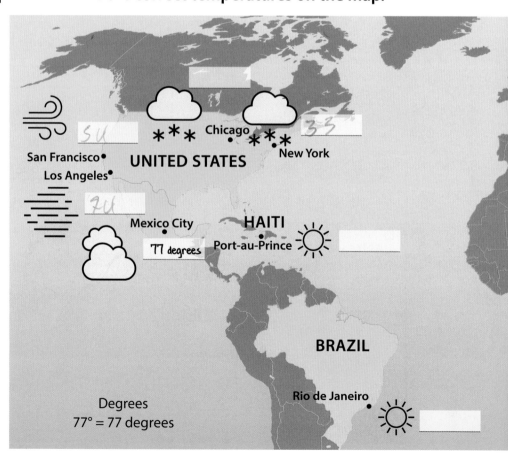

San Francisco • SU

*** Chicago

*** New York 33

UNITED STATES

Los Angeles •

7U

Mexico City HAITI

77 degrees Port-au-Prince

BRAZIL

Rio de Janeiro

Degrees
77° = 77 degrees

C. Work in pairs. Ask your partner questions about the map to fill in your chart. Then, switch roles.

EXAMPLE: Student A: How's the weather in Mexico City?
Student B: It's cloudy and 77 degrees.

Student A

City	Weather	Temperature
Mexico City	cloudy	77°
Los Angeles	foggy	
New York	snowy	
Port-au-Prince	sonny	90

Student B

City	Weather	Temperature
Tokyo		66
Moscow		50
Ho Chi Minh City		90
Rio de Janeiro	sonny	95

D. **RESEARCH** Ask about your partner's native country.

Country	Weather	Temperature

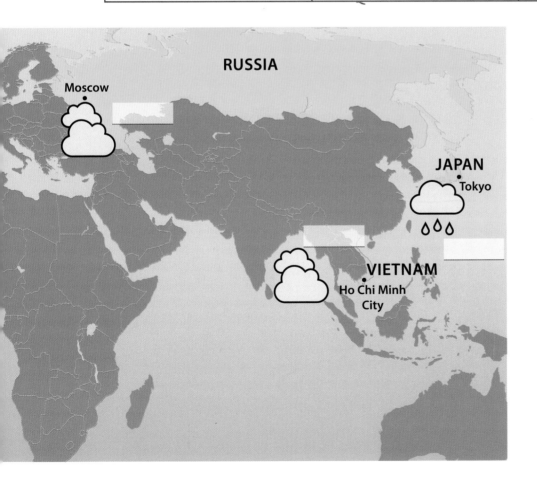

E. Write the correct word for each picture.

| sunny | rainy | cloudy | snowy | windy | foggy |

F. Practice the conversations. Use the pictures in Exercise E to make new conversations.

Student A points to the sunny picture.

Student A: How's the weather today?
Student B: It's <u>sunny</u>.

Student B points to the snowy picture.

Student B: Is it <u>cold</u> today?
Student A: <u>Yes, it is.</u>

Monedero = wallet

  **What does he look like?**

Before You Watch

A. Look at the picture and answer the questions.

1. Where are Mr. Patel and Mateo?

2. What is Mateo holding?

While You Watch

B. Write _Mr. Patel, Mateo,_ or _Timothy Roberts_ to show who completed the action.

1. He leaves the store.   _Mr. Patel_

2. He returns the wallet.   _Mr. Patel_

3. He directs a customer to the boy's section.   _Mateo_

4. He finds a wallet.   _Mateo_

5. He shakes Mr. Patel's hand.   _Mr. Patel_

Check Your Understanding

C. Write the words to describe both customers. Follow the example.

	First customer	Second customer
30s or 40s?	30s	
Blond hair or bald?	30s	
Blue shirt or red shirt?		
Khaki pants or brown pants?		

A. **Look at the information about Ivan and Anya. Answer the questions in complete sentences.**

Ivan
Married
70 years old
Moscow, Russia
Residence: California

Anya
Married
68 years old
Moscow, Russia
Residence: California

1. Where is Ivan from?

   He is from *Moscow Russia* .

2. Where do Anya and Ivan live?

   They *a californi* .

3. How old is Ivan?

   Ivan *70 years old* .

4. Who is older, Ivan or Anya?

   _____

5. Are Ivan and Anya married?

   They are married

B. **Write *live* or *lives*.**

1. Gilberto and Lien *They lives* in Los Angeles.
2. We *The* with our mother and father.
3. I *live* in California.
4. Mario *lives* in a house.
5. Lien *livis* in Vietnam in the summer and Los Angeles in the winter.
6. You *live* in the United States.

Learner Log

I can identify family relationships.   I can describe people.
☐ Yes ☐ No ☐ Maybe   ☐ Yes ☐ No ☐ Maybe

C. **Look at Anya's family tree and write the relationships.**

1. Dimitri and Nadia are _____ husband _____ and _____ wife _____.

2. Dimitri and Vladimir are _____ and _____.

3. Nadia and Natalya are _____ and _____.

4. Irina and Natalya are _____ and _____.

5. Ivan and Vladimir are _____ and _____.

D. **Describe Mario on page 20. Describe his height, weight, age, hair, and eyes.**

_____

_____

_____

_____

_____

_____

E. Write the weather words under the pictures.

1. _____   2. _____   3. _____   4. _____

F. Read Vladimir's schedule.

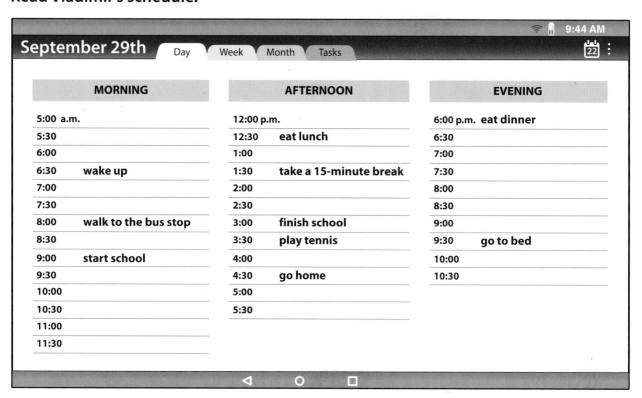

September 29th Day Week Month Tasks   9:44 AM

MORNING		AFTERNOON		EVENING	
5:00 a.m.		12:00 p.m.		6:00 p.m.	eat dinner
5:30		12:30	eat lunch	6:30	
6:00		1:00		7:00	
6:30	wake up	1:30	take a 15-minute break	7:30	
7:00		2:00		8:00	
7:30		2:30		8:30	
8:00	walk to the bus stop	3:00	finish school	9:00	
8:30		3:30	play tennis	9:30	go to bed
9:00	start school	4:00		10:00	
9:30		4:30	go home	10:30	
10:00		5:00			
10:30		5:30			
11:00					
11:30					

G. Describe Vladimir's day. Write four complete sentences.

1. _____

2. _____

3. _____

4. _____

✓ **Describe a student**

In this project, you are going to describe a student on your team or a student from the picture on page 20. You will include a family tree, a one-day planner, and a one-month calendar for the student.

1. **COLLABORATE** Form a team with four or five students. In your team, you need:

Position	Job description	Student name
Student 1: **Team Leader**	Check that everyone speaks English. Check that everyone participates.	
Student 2: **Writer**	Write a paragraph with help from the team.	
Student 3: **Artist**	Make a family tree with help from the team.	
Students 4/5: **Planners**	Make a one-day planner and a one-month calendar with help from the team.	

2. Choose a student from your team or a student from page 20 (not Kenji or Anya).

3. Write a paragraph about the student and his or her family. Answer these questions in your paragraph:

   Where is the student from?

   Where does he or she live now?

   How many brothers and sisters does he or she have?

4. Make a family tree for the student. _17_

5. Make a one-day planner for the student. _23_

6. Make a one-month calendar for the student.

7. Report to the class.

EXPLORER NEIL LOSIN

Making Science Beautiful

" … when I'm not working on my research, I'm usually working on a film or photography project to bring science to a bigger audience."
—Neil Losin

A. PREDICT Look at the picture and answer the questions.

1. Do you think Neil likes to work outside?

   a. yes   b. no

2. What do you think his job is?

   a. a writer   b. a photographer   c. a teacher   d. all of the above

3. Do you think he likes his job?

   a. yes   b. maybe   c. no

B. Write sentences about Neil.

Age: _____

Eye color: _____

Hair color: _____

C. Read about Neil Losin.

My name is Neil Losin. I'm a biologist, photographer, and filmmaker. A biologist studies life and living things. I especially like to study lizards, but I'm interested in all animals. I use my photographs and videos to tell stories. I have a company called Day's Edge Productions. My partner in the company is Nate Dappen. He's a photographer and filmmaker, too. With our films, we want to teach people about science, nature, and conservation.

I have a very busy schedule. I really don't have much free time, but I like to work. I work at the University of California, Los Angeles. When I'm in Los Angeles, I teach, do research, and write papers. I also work in Miami, Florida. When I'm in Florida, I work outside in the hot sun. I look for lizards and other small animals.

D. INFER Answer the questions.

1. Does Neil like his life? How do you know? Write a sentence from the article.

   _____

2. Do you think Neil likes animals? Write a sentence from the article.

   _____

3. Read the sentences below. Which sentence tells you that Neil's company wants to help people to learn?

   a. I have a company called Day's Edge Productions.

   b. My partner in the company is Nate Dappen.

   c. With our films, we want to teach people about science, nature, and conservation.

E. APPLY Read what Neil does every day. Then, write what you do.

Neil works at the University of California, Los Angeles. He teaches, he does research, and he writes papers.

   _____

   _____

   _____

   _____

Let's Go Shopping!

A shopkeeper shows off his hat collection.

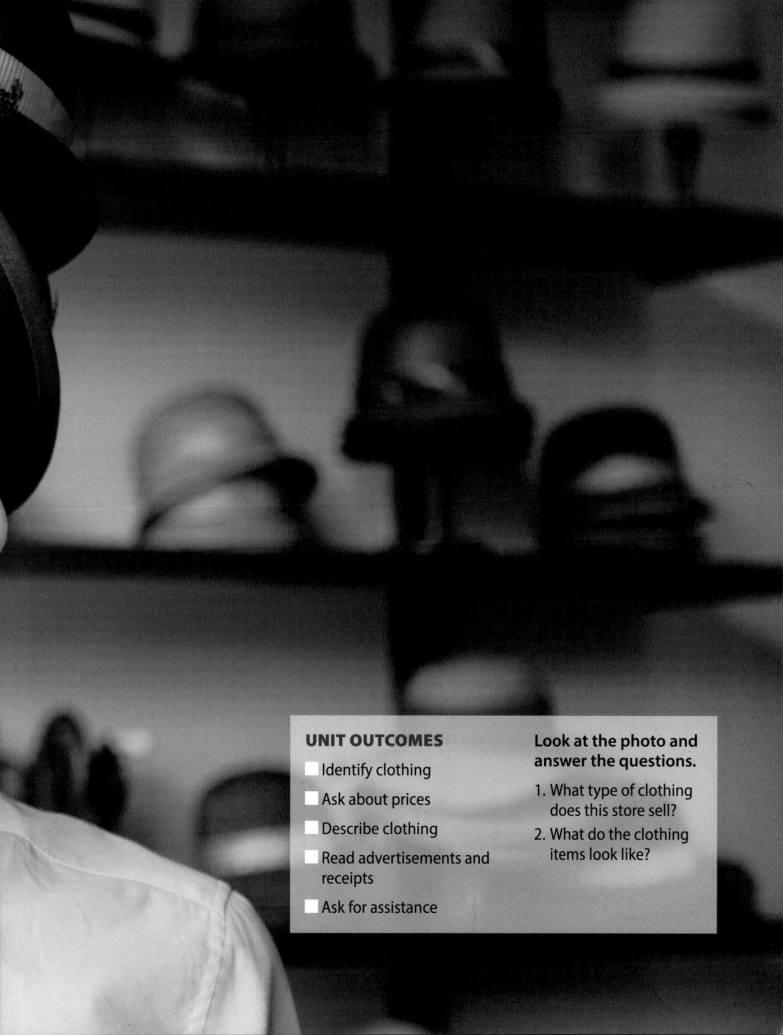

UNIT OUTCOMES

- Identify clothing
- Ask about prices
- Describe clothing
- Read advertisements and receipts
- Ask for assistance

Look at the photo and answer the questions.

1. What type of clothing does this store sell?

2. What do the clothing items look like?

GOAL ▪ Identify clothing

A. PREDICT Look at the picture and answer questions about the Hernandez family.

1. Where do you think the Hernandez family is from?

   I think the Hernandez family is from _____.

2. Which season do you think they like? Which season don't they like?

   I think they like _____.

   They don't like _____.

🎧 **B. Listen and check your answers in Exercise A.**

CD 1
TR 24

🎧 **C. CLASSIFY** Listen again and write the clothes the Hernandez family wears in the summer and the winter.

CD 1
TR 24

Clothes in the summer	Clothes in the winter
sho	coats
s.	sckay
sti	
sc	

D. Look at the picture. What clothes can you see?

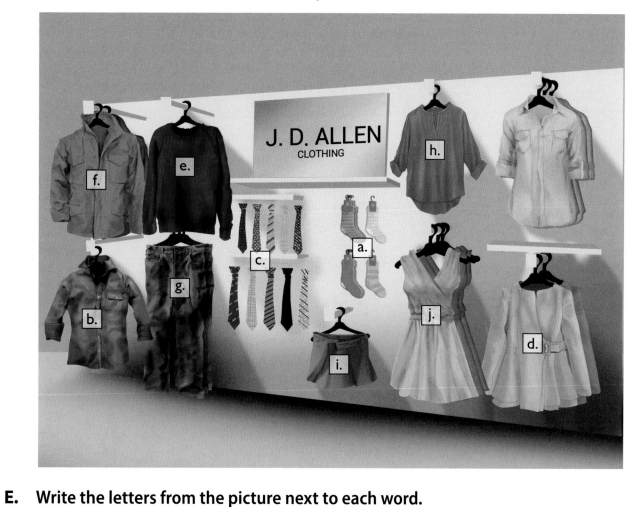

E. Write the letters from the picture next to each word.

_h_ blouses   _b_ shirts   _c_ ties   _2_ pants   _i_ skirts

_F_ coats   _e_ sweaters   _d_ jackets   _a_ socks   _j_ dresses

F. CLASSIFY In a group, list the clothes you wear in the summer and in the winter.

Summer	Winter
Skirts	
Dresses	
blouse	

G. Study the charts with your classmates and teacher.

Simple Present		
Subject	**Verb**	
I, You, We, They	wear	sweaters t-shirts shoes
He, She	wears*	
Pronunciation: */z/		

Negative Simple Present			
Subject	**Negative**	**Base verb**	
I, You, We, They	don't	wear	pants hats sandals
He, She	doesn't		

H. IDENTIFY Write sentences about Mario.

1. What does Mario wear to work?

He wears boots to work.

He, wears hat

He wear pants

2. What does Mario wear to the beach?

He wears sandals to the beach.

_____

_____

I. Talk in a group about what Mario wears to work and to the beach.

EXAMPLE: Mario wears boots to work. He wears sandals to the beach.

J. Write sentences about what you and your classmates wear to school.

1. The student next to me wears _____ to school. He/She doesn't wear

_____.

2. I wear _____ to school. I don't wear _____.

3. My classmates _____ to school. They _____.

GOAL ▪ Ask about prices

A. Look at Lien and Steve. Write the words from the box next to the clothes.

t-shirt	gloves	sunglasses	sweater	shorts
coat	scarf	boots	sandals	baseball cap

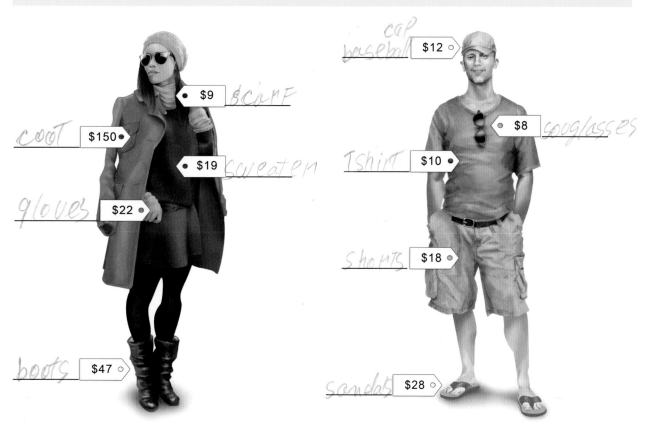

Lien's clothes (handwritten): scarf $9, coot $150, sweaten $19, gloves $22, boots $47

Steve's clothes (handwritten): baseball cap $12, sunglasses $8, Tshirt $10, Shorts $18, sandals $28

B. Practice the conversation. Use the information in Exercise A to make new conversations.

Student A: How much is Lien's <u>scarf</u>?
Student B: It's <u>$9.00</u>.
Student B: How much are the <u>sunglasses</u>?
Student A: They're <u>$8.00</u>.

C. CALCULATE What is the total cost of the clothing?

1. How much are Lien's winter clothes? _____

2. How much are Steve's summer clothes? _____

D. Study the chart with your classmates and teacher.

Comparative and Superlative Adjectives		
Adjective	Comparative adjective	Superlative adjective
cheap	cheaper	the cheapest
expensive	more expensive	the most expensive

E. **COMPARE** In pairs, ask your partner about the prices of clothes in Exercise A and write them below.

Ask your partner about Lien's clothes for winter.

Student A: How much is the coat?

Student B: It's $150.00.

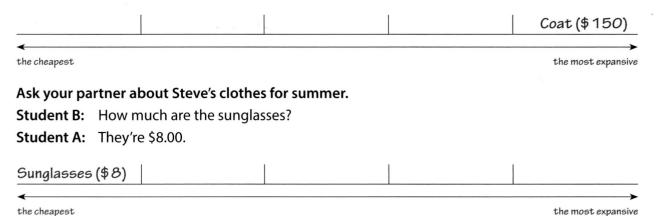

				Coat ($150)

the cheapest   the most expansive

Ask your partner about Steve's clothes for summer.

Student B: How much are the sunglasses?

Student A: They're $8.00.

Sunglasses ($8)			

the cheapest   the most expansive

F. **ORGANIZE** Listen to the conversations. Write the clothing on a piece of paper. Then, put the clothing in order from the cheapest to the most expensive in the table below.

CD 1
TR 25–27

	Clothing	Price
the cheapest	Pants	$22
	Sneakers	$15
	gloves	$10
	Socks	$3
	Scarf	$25
the most expensive	cap	$18.

G. INTERPRET Answer questions about the receipts.

RECEIPT		RECEIPT		RECEIPT
Dress $88.89		Suit $299.99		Shoes $34.99
Tax $7.11		Tax $23.92		Tax $2.80
TOTAL $96.00		TOTAL $323.91		TOTAL $37.79
Customer Copy		Customer Copy		Customer Copy

1. How much is the dress? _It's $88.89_

2. How much is the tax for the suit? _The tax $7.11_

3. How much is the total for the shoes? _The Total $96.00_

H. Practice the conversation. Use the receipts in Exercise G to make new conversations.

Customer: Excuse me. How much is the dress?
Salesperson: It's $88.89.
Customer: How much is it with tax?
Salesperson: It's $96.00 with tax.
Customer: Great! / No, thanks. That's too expensive.

I. APPLY What clothing do you need? You have $300. Look at some online stores, make a list, and share it with the class.

Sales clerks can tell you the price of items.

GOAL ▊ Describe clothing

A. **Look at the sizes, colors, patterns, and styles of the clothes in the picture.**

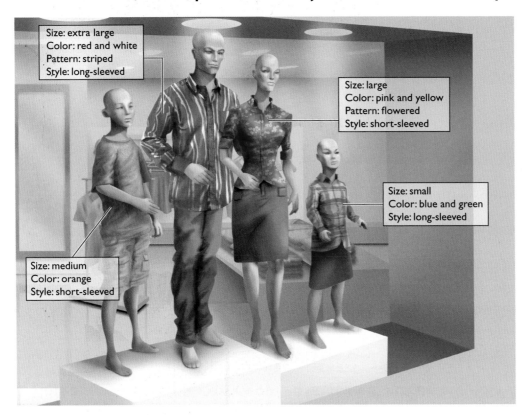

Size: extra large
Color: red and white
Pattern: striped
Style: long-sleeved

Size: large
Color: pink and yellow
Pattern: flowered
Style: short-sleeved

Size: small
Color: blue and green
Style: long-sleeved

Size: medium
Color: orange
Style: short-sleeved

CD 1
TR 28

B. **IDENTIFY** **Listen and write the names of the Nguyen brothers.**

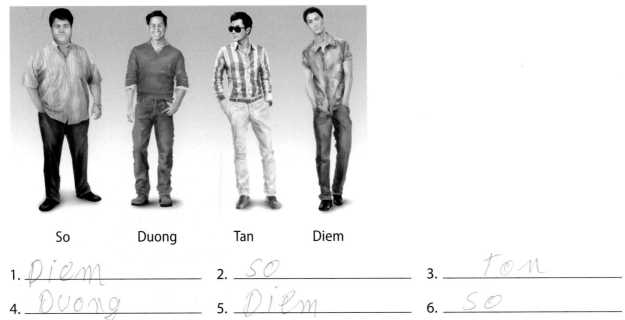

So   Duong   Tan   Diem

1. _Diem_   2. _So_   3. _ton_

4. _Duong_   5. _Diem_   6. _So_

C. Study the chart with your classmates and teacher.

Present Continuous			
Subject	*Be*	Verb + *-ing*	Example sentence
I	am		I **am wearing** a sweater right now.
You, We, They	are	wearing	We **are wearing** shoes.
He, She, It	is		She **is wearing** sunglasses today.

D. Complete the sentences with the present continuous form of *wear*.

1. He _is wearing_ a flowered shirt.

2. The woman _is wearing_ a beautiful dress.

3. They _are wearing_ new clothes.

4. Alan and I _am wearing_ sunglasses.

5. You _are wearing_ a flowered blouse.

6. I _am wearing_ a striped shirt.

E. Write two sentences about each Nguyen brother from Exercise B.

1. *So is wearing an extra-large, blue, striped shirt.*

_____

2. _Duang is wearing a long red sweater_
He is wearing blue jeans and brown boots

3. _Ton is wearing long sleeven_
striped red and white shirt

4. _Diem is wearing green pants_
Hi is wearing a short sleeve flowered
shirt

F. Look at the ad and describe what the people are wearing.

G. Practice the conversation. Use the ad in Exercise F to make new conversations.

Student A: What is this man wearing in this picture? (points to picture)
Student B: He is wearing a black suit and a red tie.

H. **APPLY** Write sentences about what you and your partner are wearing.

1. I _____.

2. I _____.

3. I _____.

4. I _____.

5. My partner _____.

6. My partner _____.

7. My partner _____.

8. My partner _____.

GOAL   Read advertisements and receipts

A. **PREDICT** Read the advertisement and guess the sale price. Then, listen and fill in the missing information.

SALE COUPON
★ ★ ★
Valid Tuesday, Wednesday, and Thursday *only*

SALE

SAM'S UNIFORM COMPANY

SAM'S UNIFORM COMPANY

Men's Shirts, Regular Price: $26.00
Sale Price: _3 0_   You save: _4_

Women's Pants, Regular Price: $45.00
Sale Price: _36_   You save: _9_

Sneakers, Regular Price: $22.00
Sale Price: _15.40_   You save: _6.60_

Baseball Caps, Regular Price: $23.00
Sale Price: _20_   You save: _3_

SHOP NOW AND SAVE!

B. Listen again and check (✓) the clothing that needs a coupon.

____✓ 1. men's shirts   ____ 2. women's pants   ____ 3. sneakers   ____✓ 4. baseball caps

C. Practice the conversation with a partner. Then, use the ad in Exercise A to make new conversations.

Salesperson:	Can I help you?
Customer:	How much are the <u>shirts</u>?
Salesperson:	The shirts are <u>$26.00</u>.
Customer:	The ad says they are <u>$4.00</u> off.
Salesperson:	Sorry. You're right. They are <u>$22.00</u>.

> *OFF*
> Read how *off* is used to talk about savings.
> The shirts are $4.00 off.
> They are $4.00 off with a coupon.
> They are $4.00 off the regular price.

D. INTERPRET Read the receipt and circle the correct answers. Then, use the advertisement in Exercise A to complete the receipt. Use the sale price of each item.

Sam's Uniform Company
20 Row St., Chicago,
IL 80000

Item	Quantity	Unit Price	Total
Men's shirts	3	$	$66
Women's pants	2	$	$72
Men's boots	1	$37.00	$37
Women's belts	2	$18.00	$36
		Grand Total	$211

Sales tax of 10.25% included

Tel: (312) 555-6789
Website: samsunif0rmc0.com

1. How many shirts are on the receipt?

_____

2. What does *unit price* mean?
   a. how many
   b. how much for one
   c. total price

3. What does *item* mean?
   a. the price
   b. how many
   c. kind of clothing

4. What does *grand total* mean?
   a. price for all items
   b. coupon price
   c. number of items

E. CALCULATE Complete the receipt.

Addy's Clothing Company
25 First St., Chicago,
IL 80000

Item	Quantity	Unit Price	Total
Men's shirts	2	$32.00	$64
Women's pants	4	$34.00	$136
Men's boots	1	$48.00	$48
Women's belts	1	$16.00	$16
		Grand Total	$264

Sales tax of 10.25% included

Website: addyscl0thingc0.com

F. Read the paragraph. Why does Alexi shop at Addy's Clothing Company?

I shop at Addy's because it's close to my house on First Street. Addy's has good prices. The prices at Sam's are also good, but it's far away. I think they have boots on sale for $37. Addy's boots are more expensive, but I don't need boots right now. Maybe they will be on sale in the future.

G. COMPARE Look at the receipts in exercises D and E. Complete the graph about Sam's Uniform Company and Addy's Clothing Company.

COMPARISON SHOPPING

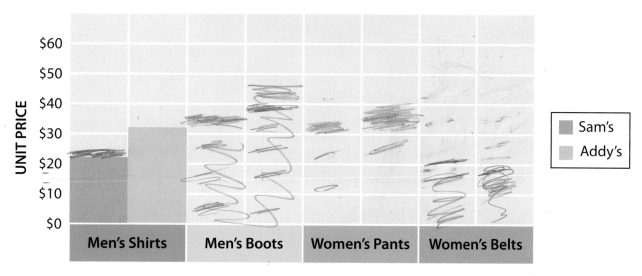

H. APPLY Visit two clothing stores near your home or on the Internet. Choose one item of clothing and compare the prices. Report to the class.

Comparing prices is as important as comparing styles and colors.

LESSON ⑤ Which one do you want?

GOAL ■ Ask for assistance

A. Look at the picture. Where is Roberto? Who is he talking to?

🎧 B. Listen to the conversation between Roberto and the salesperson.

CD 1
TR 30

Roberto:	Excuse me. Can you help me?
Salesperson:	Sure. What can I do for you?
Roberto:	I want a <u>cap</u> and a few other things.
Salesperson:	What color do you want? We have an assortment.
Roberto:	I want this <u>black</u> one, but it is too expensive.
Salesperson:	Oh, I'm sorry. Maybe a <u>yellow</u> one?
Roberto:	I prefer <u>orange</u>.

🎧 C. DISTINGUISH Listen to the conversations. Circle the items Roberto wants.

CD 1
TR 31-34

1. orange cap	red cap	blue cap	yellow cap
2. green umbrella	blue umbrella	black umbrella	red umbrella
3. gray jeans	brown jeans	blue jeans	black jeans
4. white socks	brown socks	black socks	yellow socks

D. Make a conversation between Roberto and the salesperson using the information in Exercise C.

E. Study the chart with your classmates and teacher.

	Near	Not Near
Singular	this	that
Plural	these	those

F. Look at the picture. Fill in the blanks with *this, that, these,* or *those.*

1. _____That_____ cap is yellow and _____This_____ cap is orange.
2. _____This_____ umbrella is _____That_____ and
   _____This_____ umbrella is green.
3. _____Those_____ jeans are blue and _____These_____ jeans are
   _____blak_____.
4. _____These_____ socks are _____white_____ and
   _____Those_____ socks are yellow.

G. Practice the conversation. Use *this, that, these,* or *those* to make new conversations.

Student A: What color is *that* shirt?
Student B: It's purple.
Student B: What color are *these* pants?
Student A: They're black.

H. Look at the reasons for returning clothing.

> I don't like the color.
>
> It is damaged.
>
> It doesn't fit.
>
> I don't like it.
>
> It is the wrong size.

I. Read and listen to the conversation.

CD 1
TR 35

Manager:	May I help you?
Roberto:	Yes, I want to return these jeans.
Manager:	Yes, sir. Why do you want to return them?
Roberto:	They don't fit.
Manager:	OK. Do you have the receipt?
Roberto:	Oh, no, I don't.
Manager:	I'm sorry, you can't return them without a receipt, but you can exchange them.
Roberto:	OK. Maybe I will get those brown ones over there.
Manager:	That's fine, sir.

J. Practice new conversations with a partner. Return the items below.

> blouse / damaged
>
> shoes / don't fit
>
> shorts / don't like
>
> dress / wrong size

SINGULAR AND PLURAL	
Singular	**Plural**
return it	return them
exchange it	exchange them

Manager:	May I help you?
Customer:	Yes, I want to return *This blouse*.
Manager:	Of course. Why do you want to return *it*?
Customer:	*It's damaged*

K. CREATE Imagine that you need to return something. Write a new conversation with a partner and perform it for the class.

▶ # Do you have the receipt?

Before You Watch

A. Look at the picture and answer the questions.

1. Where are Hector and Mrs. Smith?

2. What is Mrs. Smith doing?

While You Watch

B. ▶ Watch the video and complete the dialog.

Mateo: Hello, Mrs. Smith. Is everything OK?

Mrs. Smith: Well, I want to (1) _____return_____ this sweater, but I don't have the receipt. It was a present.

Mateo: Oh, I see. Well, you can (2) _che cho_ it for something else in the store. Do you see anything you'd like in the store?

Mrs. Smith: Actually … I really like that (3) _blowse_ over there.

Mateo: Well, maybe you can exchange this (4) _swepe_ for that blouse over there.

Hector: Here you are, Mrs. Smith. This looks just your (5) _zise_.

Check Your Understanding

C. Read the statements. Write *T* for true and *F* for false.

1. Hector doesn't know how to use the cash register. _T_

2. Mateo takes a break. _T_

3. Hector tells Mrs. Smith she is his first customer. _T_

4. Mrs. Smith wants to return a green sweater. _F_

5. Mateo tells Mrs. Smith she can exchange the sweater for something else. _F_

6. Mrs. Smith tells Mr. Patel she is not happy with the service at the shop. _F_

Review

Learner Log

I can identify clothing.
☑Yes ☑No ☑Maybe

I can describe clothing.
☑Yes ☐No ☑Maybe

A. Look at the advertisements.

1.

SALE PRICE $14
REGULAR PRICE $28
SIZE M AND L ONLY

2.

ALL SIZES AND COLORS
SALE PRICE $15
WITH COUPON
REGULAR PRICE $25

3.

COUPON REQUIRED
SALE PRICE $45
REGULAR PRICE $52
SMALL SIZES ONLY

4.

NO COUPON REQUIRED
SALE PRICE $22
REGULAR PRICE $25
ALL SIZES

5.

ALL SIZES
SALE PRICE $24
SAVINGS $5
NO COUPON NECESSARY

6.

ALL SIZES AND COLORS
SALE PRICE $34
WITH COUPON
REGULAR PRICE $44

B. Fill in the information using the advertisements in Exercise A.

1. Item: _____
   Need Coupon? _no_
   Color: _blue_
   Style: _shon seeve_
   Size: _____
   Sale Price: $ _14_
   Regular Price: $ _28_
   Savings: $ _14_

2. Item: _shirt_
   Need Coupon? _yes_
   Color: _____
   Style: _long seev_
   Size: _L m_
   Sale Price: $ _15_
   Regular Price: $ _10_
   Savings: $ _15_

3. Item: _dress_
   Need Coupon? _yes_
   Color: _red_
   Size: _small on 11_
   Sale Price: $ _45_
   Regular Price: $ _52_
   Savings: $ _7_

4. Item: _pont_
   Need Coupon? _no_
   Color: _blu jen_
   Size: _____
   Sale Price: $ _22_
   Regular Price: $ _25_
   Savings: $ _25_

5. Item: _snicol_
   Need Coupon? _no_
   Color: _blak_
   Size: _8_
   Sale Price: $ _24_
   Regular Price: $ _5_
   Savings: $ _20_

6. Item: _choes_
   Need Coupon? _yes_
   Color: _pink_
   Size: _nine_
   Sale Price: $ _34_
   Regular Price: $ _44_
   Savings: $ _10_

Learner Log

I can read advertisements and receipts.   I can ask about prices.
■Yes ■No ■Maybe   ■Yes ■No ■Maybe

C. Read the receipts and answer the questions.

Lana's BOUTIQUE

Women's boots..............$32.55
Women's pants............$24.50
Belt..............................$18.95
Blouse $32.50

TOTAL $108.50

Clothing for Less

Women's boots...............$28.55
Women's pants...............$30.00
Belt..................................$12.95
Blouse $28.50

TOTAL $100.00
Customer Copy

THE TRUE Shopper

Women's boots............... $40.00
Women's pants..............$34.00
Belt..................................$24.50
Blouse $26.95

TOTAL $125.45
No Refunds without Receipt

1. Which store has the cheapest total? _____

2. Where are blouses the cheapest? _____

3. Where are blouses the most expensive? _____

4. Which store has women's pants cheaper than *Clothing for Less?* _____

5. Which store has blouses more expensive than *Clothing for Less?* _____

6. Which do you think is the best store? _____

D. Complete the sentences with the present continuous form of *wear*.

1. Maria _____*is wearing*_____ red pants and a pink blouse.

2. Alan _____ new shoes and socks.

3. Marjorie and Paula _____ beautiful dresses.

4. The children _____ shorts.

5. I _____ a suit and tie.

6. We _____ coats.

7. She _____ a new scarf.

E. **Write three things you can say if you want to make a return.**

1. _____

2. _____

3. _____

F. **Look at the picture. Complete the sentences below with *this, that, these,* or *those.***

1. _____ white shirt is perfect. I don't want _____ blue one.

2. _____ white shoes are great, but I think I want _____ blue ones.

3. _____ shirt is cheap. _____ shirt is better, but it is too expensive.

4. _____ table has white shoes on it.

G. **Write what you and your partner are wearing right now.**

You: _____

_____

_____

Your partner: _____

_____

_____

TEAM PROJECT ✓ Design a clothing store

In this project, you are going to design your own clothing store and create an advertisement for it.

1. **COLLABORATE** Form a team with four or five students. In your team, you need:

Position	Job description	Student name
Student 1: **Team Leader**	Check that everyone speaks English. Check that everyone participates.	
Student 2: **Artist**	Design an advertisement with help from the team.	
Student 3: **Sales Specialist**	Write a conversation and practice it with your team.	
Students 4/5: **Spokespeople**	Prepare a class presentation with help from the team.	

2. Choose a name for your store. What do you sell? Women's clothes? Men's clothes? Children's clothes?

3. Make a list of clothing you sell on a piece of paper. List at least eight items. Describe the clothing by size, color, pattern, and price. Are your clothes for work, sports, or school?

4. Draw or find and cut out pictures of the clothing items in your store. Make a newspaper advertisement for your store using the pictures of the items.

5. Practice asking for prices, selling clothing, and returning clothing with your teammates.

6. Present your advertisement to the class.

People are finding creative ways to create stores. This mobile clothing store uses social media to tell customers where it will be.

EXPLORER CONRAD ANKER

The Right Gear for the Job

"The mountaineer suit is like a sleeping bag with arms and legs on it."
—Conrad Anker

A. CLASSIFY Put the clothing from the box in the correct columns. Then, add two more words to each column.

| t-shirt | sandals | jacket | gloves | shorts | boots |

Cold weather clothing	Warm weather clothing

B. DISCUSS In a group, talk about what temperatures are *very cold, cold, warm, very warm,* and *hot.*

Very cold	Cold	Warm	Very warm	Hot
_____ degrees	_____ degrees	_____ degrees	_____ degrees	_____ degrees

C. Read about Conrad Anker.

Conrad Anker is a rock climber. He has climbed some of the most challenging mountains in the world. The tallest mountain on Earth is Mount Everest and Conrad has climbed it three times. Some people say that Conrad is a legend. A legend is a very famous person. He is often a little embarrassed when people say this about him.

Conrad speaks to other climbers and gives them advice about what to take when they climb mountains like Everest. The proper clothing is not cheap. It is sometimes very expensive. People don't wear sandals or t-shirts when they climb tall mountains. Conrad suggests double boots. A double boot is a boot inside a boot. He also suggests mittens. Mittens are like gloves with no fingers, only a thumb. He also suggests a special mountaineer suit. Conrad says a mountaineer suit is like a sleeping bag with arms and legs.

The average temperature at the top of Mount Everest when people climb in May is minus four degrees Fahrenheit. It is dangerous to climb high mountains, but with proper training and advice, people can do it.

D. ANALYZE Draw lines from the new words to the definitions.

legend	gloves with no fingers
double boot	a sleeping bag with arms and legs
mittens	a famous person
mountaineer suit	a boot inside another boot

E. Write the full sentence from the article for each definition.

1. legend = A legend is a very famous person.

2. double boot = _____

3. mittens = _____

4. mountaineer suit = _____

F. APPLY What clothes do you wear in the winter? Make a list on a separate piece of paper.

Food and Nutrition

Elementary schoolchildren make
healthy choices.

UNIT OUTCOMES

☐ Read a menu

☐ Make a shopping list

☐ Locate items in a supermarket

☐ Identify healthy foods

☐ Read recipes

Look at the photo and answer the questions.

1. What food can you see?

2. Where can you find this food in a supermarket?

LESSON **1** Augustin's restaurant

GOAL ▪ Read a menu

A. PREDICT Look at the picture. Where is Gabriel? What is his job?

🎧 **B.** Close your book and listen to Gabriel's story. Then, open your book and read.

CD 1
TR 36

> My name is Gabriel. I'm a cook in my father's restaurant. His name is Augustin. My mother, sister, and brother work here, too. We have American food in our restaurant. I want to have some food from other countries, too. Maybe someday we can have an international restaurant.

C. Circle the correct answers.

1. Gabriel works in a restaurant.	~~True~~	False
2. Gabriel only cooks American food in his father's restaurant.	~~True~~	False
3. His sister doesn't work in the restaurant.	True	~~False~~
4. He wants the restaurant to have food from different countries.	~~True~~	False

62 Unit 3

D. **INTERPRET** Look at the menu. What do you want for lunch? Complete the guest check.

Table No.	Check No.
	200345

GUEST CHECK

Table No.	Check No.
	200345

Dinner salad	$ 1.85
Rice	$ 1.25
Tea	$ 1.75
cheesecake	$ 2.00
Milk	$ 1.29
Total:	$ 5.04

CD 1
TR 37–39

E. **CALCULATE** Listen to the people ordering food in a restaurant. Write down the orders and calculate the cost.

Table No. 1	Check No. 1001

GUEST CHECK

Table No. 1	Check No. 1001

1	Super burger combo	$ 5.99
1	Dinner salad	$ 1.85
		$
		$
		$
	Total:	$ 7.87

Table No. 2	Check No. 1002

GUEST CHECK

Table No. 2	Check No. 1002

2	ciRloin	$
2	vegetoble	$
		$
		$
		$
	Total:	$

Table No. 3	Check No. 1003

GUEST CHECK

Table No. 3	Check No. 1003

Cesar	$ 2.49
Milk	$ 1.29
Fresh	$ 2.00
	$
	$
Total:	$ 5.78

F. **Study the chart with your classmates and teacher.**

Questions with *Can*			
Can	Pronoun	Base verb	Example question
Can	I		Can I take your order? Can I help you?
Can	you	take help	Can you take my order? Can you take our order, please? Can you help me? Can you help us?

G. **Practice the conversation. Use the menu in Exercise D to make new conversations.**

Server: Can I take your order?

Customer: Yes, I want a <u>Caesar salad</u>, please.

H. **CREATE** **In a group, make a menu. Include food from your country.**

Mi Casa Retaurron			
Soups and Salads	Price	Side Orders	Price
Vetobos soops	$ 4.25	_____	$ ____
potelosaladd	$ 3.145	_____	$ ____
Sandwiches	Price	Beverages	Price
_____	$ ____	_____	$ ____
_____	$ ____	_____	$ ____
Main Courses	Price	Desserts	Price
_____	$ ____	_____	$ ____
_____	$ ____	_____	$ ____

LESSON **2** Do we need carrots?

GOAL ■ Make a shopping list

A. PREDICT Look at the picture. What are Augustin and Silvia doing?

B. Read the paragraph.

> Augustin and Silvia make a shopping list for the restaurant every Thursday morning. On Thursdays, they are not busy. They already have a lot of food this week. They don't need to buy very much.

C. Listen to Augustin and Silvia make their shopping list. Check (✓) each item they need.

CD 1
TR 40

☑ ground beef   ☐ turkey   ☐ ham

☐ bacon   ☐ tuna fish   ☐ chicken

☐ lettuce   ☐ tomatoes   ☐ carrots

☐ fresh fruit   ☐ sugar   ☐ flour

D. Write sentences about what Augustin and Silvia need and don't need.

1. They need ground beef.

2. They don't need _____ .

3. _____

4. _____

5. _____

E. IDENTIFY Complete Augustin's shopping list with the words from the pictures.

carton(s)

box(es)

jar(s)

pound(s)

bag(s)

bottle(s)

can(s)

gallon(s)

loaf (loaves)

Shopping List

milk 3 _gallons_	ground beef 2 _____
flour 2 _____	sugar 3 _____
tomatoes 5 _____	jam 1 _____
bread 3 _____	oil 2 _____
cake mix 2 _____	oranges 3 _____
ice cream 4 _____	chicken soup 4 _____

Some / any	
Question	Do we need **any** milk?
Statement	We need **some** milk.

PLURALS		
/z/		/ez/
cartons	loaves	boxes
pounds	bags	
jars	cans	
bottles	gallons	

F. Practice the conversation with a partner. Use items from the shopping list to make new conversations.

Augustin: Do we need any <u>milk</u> at the store?
Silvia: Yes, we need some <u>milk</u>.
Augustin: How many <u>gallons</u> do we need?
Silvia: We need <u>three gallons</u>.

G. Study the chart with your classmates and teacher.

Count and Noncount Nouns		
Count nouns	Use *many* with nouns you can count.	How *many* tomatoes do we need? How *many* pounds of tomatoes do we need?
Noncount nouns	Use *much* with nouns you cannot count.	How *much* flour do we need? How *much* rice do we need?

H. Complete the sentences with *much* or *many*.

1. How _____ bananas do we need?

2. How _____ bottles of oil do we need?

3. How _____ oil do we need?

4. How _____ flour do we need?

5. How _____ apples do we need?

6. How _____ pounds of apples do we need?

I. **PLAN** You are planning a party for twenty people. In a group, make a shopping list on a separate piece of paper.

J. **APPLY** Go to a local market or on the Internet to find the total cost of your food items in Exercise I.

Some people get creative with their party food. What food items can you see here?

LESSON ③ At the supermarket

GOAL ▮ Locate items in a supermarket

A. CLASSIFY Look at the pictures and complete the table below.

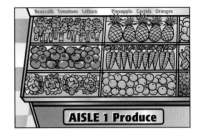

Item	Section	Aisle
flour	Baking Needs	4
milk		
tomatoes		
chicken		

The Verb *Be*	
Singular	Where **is** the flour? It **is** (it's) in Aisle 4.
Plural	Where **are** the oranges? They **are** (they're) in Aisle 1.

B. Practice the conversation with a partner. Make new conversations with *milk, tomatoes, canned corn, chicken, pears, ice cream, butter, soup, sugar,* and *oranges.*

Augustin: Excuse me. Where is <u>the flour</u>?
Store Clerk: It's in <u>Aisle 4.</u>
Augustin: Where are <u>the oranges</u>?
Store Clerk: They are in <u>Aisle 1.</u>

C. INTERPRET Read the store directory.

Product	Section	Aisle	Product	Section	Aisle	Product	Section	Aisle
Apples	*Produce*	1	Cheese	*Dairy*	5	Ice cream	*Frozen Foods*	5
Bread	*Bakery*	2	Chicken	*Meats*	8	Lettuce	*Produce*	1
Brown sugar	*Baking Needs*	4	Cookies	*Bakery*	2	Milk	*Dairy*	5
Butter	*Dairy*	5	Cream	*Dairy*	5	Oranges	*Produce*	1
Cake	*Bakery*	2	Cucumbers	*Produce*	1	Pears	*Produce*	1
Cake mix	*Baking Needs*	4	Eggs	*Bakery*	5	Soup	*Canned Goods*	3
Canned corn	*Canned Goods*	3	Flour	*Baking Needs*	4	Sugar	*Baking Needs*	4
Canned peas	*Canned Goods*	3	Ground beef	*Meats*	8	Turkey	*Meats*	8
Cantaloupe	*Produce*	1	Ham	*Meats*	8	Yogurt	*Dairy*	5

D. Answer the questions with complete sentences.

1. Where are the cookies? _They are in the Bakery section in Aisle 2._ _____

2. Where is the brown sugar? _____

3. Where is the ground beef? _____

4. Where are the eggs? _____

> **RHYTHM**
> —— · · —— ·
> Where are the cook ies?

E. Practice the conversation with a partner. Use the directory in Exercise C to make new conversations.

Augustin: Can you help me? I'm looking for the <u>canned corn</u>.
Store Clerk: It's in the <u>Canned Goods</u> section.
Augustin: Where's the <u>Canned Goods</u> section?
Store Clerk: It's in <u>Aisle 3</u>.
Augustin: Thanks!

F. PREDICT Read the shopping list. Predict which section each item is in. Then, listen to the conversation and complete the table.

CD 1
TR 41

Shopping list	Section	Aisle
beets		
muffins		
orange juice		
chicken breasts		

G. BRAINSTORM In a group, complete the cluster diagram with items from your local supermarket.

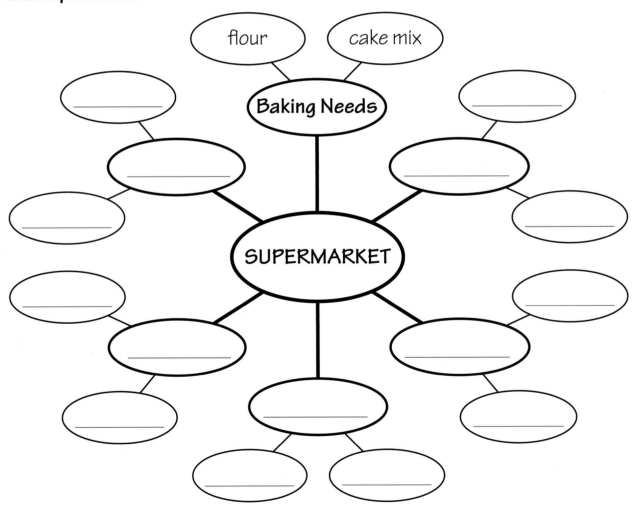

GOAL Identify healthy foods

A. Close your books and listen. Then, read about nutrition and discuss the paragraph with the class.

CD 1
TR 42

> Nutrition means the food we eat and how much we eat of each food group. Good nutrition is important. When we eat good food, our bodies are stronger and we stay healthy. MyPlate is a guide that helps us choose the best foods for a balanced diet. It is healthy to eat food from each of the main food groups.

B. INTERPRET Look at the MyPlate nutrition guide. What foods can you put into the different groups?

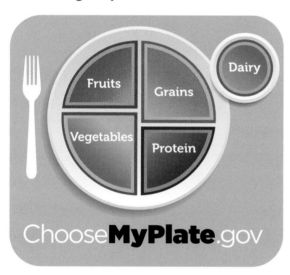

C. CLASSIFY Write nutritious foods for each category.

Grains	Vegetables	Fruits	Protein	Dairy

D. Augustin and his family don't eat together because they are very busy. Read what they eat.

Silvia

Breakfast: cereal and milk
Lunch: green salad and fruit juice
Dinner: spaghetti with meatballs, and ice cream

Augustin

Breakfast: coffee
Lunch: sausage, beans, rice, and water
Dinner: cheese, bread, green salad, and fruit

Fernando

Breakfast: fruit, cereal, milk, and toast
Lunch: pepperoni pizza and milk
Dinner: fried chicken and a baked potato

Rosa

Breakfast: toast and coffee
Lunch: soup, bread, fruit, and yogurt
Dinner: turkey, potatoes, green salad, and water

Gabriel

Breakfast: doughnut and coffee
Lunch: hamburger, fries, and soda
Dinner: pepperoni pizza and beer

SIMPLE PRESENT: HAVE

I **have** . . .
You **have** . . .
He/She **has** . . .

E. RANK Who has the best diet? In a group, rank the family members in order from the best diet to the worst. *1* is the best.

_____ Silvia

_____ Augustin

_____ Fernando

_____ Rosa

_____ Gabriel

F. COMPARE Complete the diagram. Write the foods Rosa and Augustin eat for breakfast, lunch, and dinner.

Rosa

toast

_____

_____

_____

_____

Both

coffee

_____

_____

_____

_____

Augustin

sausage

_____

_____

_____

G. APPLY What do you and your family eat for breakfast, lunch, and dinner? Complete the chart.

Breakfast	Lunch	Dinner

H. Ask a partner.

1. What do you eat for breakfast? _____

2. What do you eat for lunch? _____

3. What do you eat for dinner? _____

GOAL ▪ Read recipes

A. **INTERPRET** **Read the recipe.**

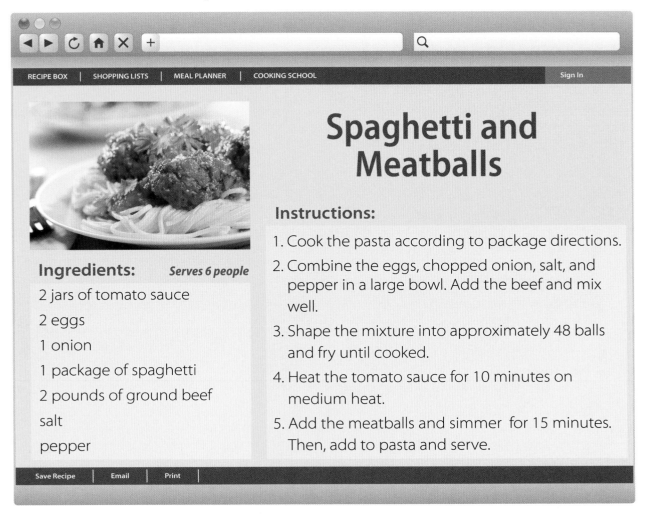

RECIPE BOX | SHOPPING LISTS | MEAL PLANNER | COOKING SCHOOL   Sign In

Spaghetti and Meatballs

Ingredients: *Serves 6 people*

2 jars of tomato sauce

2 eggs

1 onion

1 package of spaghetti

2 pounds of ground beef

salt

pepper

Instructions:

1. Cook the pasta according to package directions.

2. Combine the eggs, chopped onion, salt, and pepper in a large bowl. Add the beef and mix well.

3. Shape the mixture into approximately 48 balls and fry until cooked.

4. Heat the tomato sauce for 10 minutes on medium heat.

5. Add the meatballs and simmer for 15 minutes. Then, add to pasta and serve.

Save Recipe | Email | Print |

> *HOW MUCH? / HOW MANY?*
>
> **How many** eggs do we need?
>
> **How much** sauce do we need?

B. **Practice the conversation. Use the recipe in Exercise A to make new conversations.**

Student A: How much tomato sauce do we need?

Student B: We need two jars.

Student A: How many?

Student B: Two jars.

C. Read the recipe for mashed potatoes. Underline the new words.

Mashed Potatoes

Ingredients: *Serves 6 people*

6 potatoes
1/4 cup of milk
2 tablespoons of butter or margarine
1 teaspoon of salt
garlic salt to taste

Instructions:

1. Peel and chop potatoes.
2. Boil water. Add potatoes to boiling water.
3. Cook for 10 minutes.
4. Drain. Mix all ingredients.
5. Whip with a whisk or blender.

D. **SEQUENCE** Match the pictures with the words by drawing a line. Then, order the steps by writing numbers under the pictures.

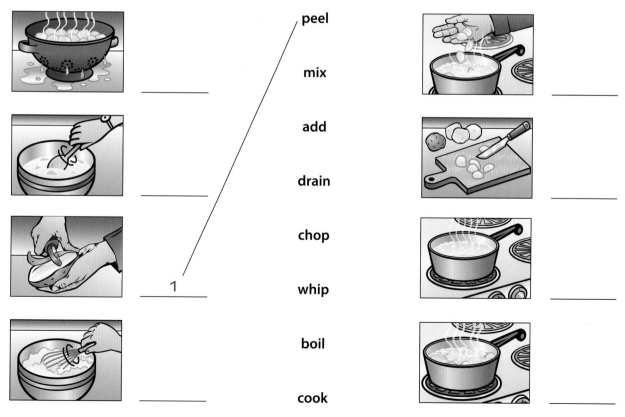

peel

mix

add

drain

chop

whip

boil

cook

E. **Study the charts with your classmates and teacher.**

Imperatives		
	Base verb	**Example sentence**
	drain	**Drain** the water.
~~you~~	chop	**Chop** the potatoes.
	peel	**Peel** the potatoes.

Negative Imperatives			
	Negative	**Base verb**	**Example sentence**
		boil	**Do not boil** the water. (**Don't boil** the water.)
~~you~~	do not don't	use	**Do not use** salt. (**Don't use** salt.)
		cook	**Do not cook** in the microwave. (**Don't cook** in the microwave.)

🎧 **F.** **SEQUENCE** **Listen to the instructions. Number them in the correct order.**

CD 1
TR 43

1. **Recipe: Cake**

    _____ Bake for 35 minutes.

    _____ Combine cake mix, water, oil, and eggs in a large bowl.

    __1__ Heat oven to 350 degrees.

    _____ Pour mixture into a pan.

2. **Recipe: Tacos**

    _____ Add ground beef, cheese, tomatoes, and lettuce to the fried tortillas.

    _____ Cut tomatoes, onions, cheese, and lettuce.

    _____ Drain grease.

    _____ Fry corn tortillas.

    _____ Fry ground beef.

G. **CREATE** **In a group, write a recipe on a separate piece of paper.**

 # Let's make a shopping list

Before You Watch

A. Look at the picture and answer the questions.

1. Where are Hector and Mrs. Sanchez?

2. What is Hector doing?

While You Watch

B. ▶ Watch the video. Circle the items Mrs. Sanchez needs to buy.

1. two pounds of ground beef   2. a dozen eggs

3. an onion   4. garlic

5. a green bell pepper   6. ketchup

7. breadcrumbs   8. milk

9. salt and pepper   10. oregano

11. basil   12. ice cream

Check Your Understanding

C. Show the correct order of events by writing a number next to each sentence.

1. _____ Hector reminds his mother to buy ice cream.

2. _____ Mrs. Sanchez reads her list and Hector checks to see if they have the items.

3. _____ Hector agrees to help his mother with a shopping list.

4. _____ Mrs. Sanchez thanks Hector and leaves.

5. _____ Hector enters the kitchen where his mother is writing a list.

Review

Learner Log

I can read a menu.
☐ Yes ☐ No ☐ Maybe

I can make a shopping list.
☐ Yes ☐ No ☐ Maybe

A. Look at the menu. Fill in the name of each section.

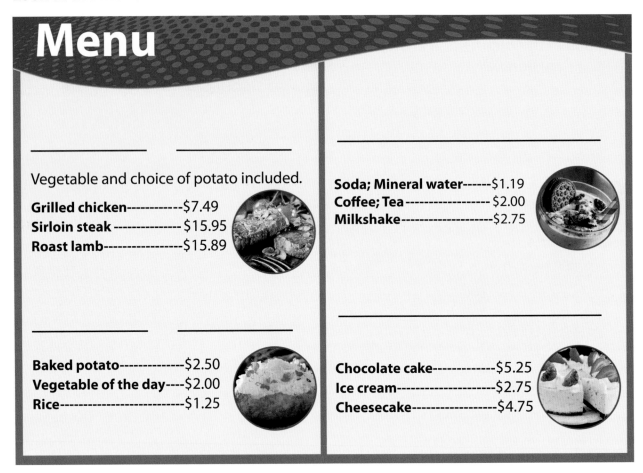

Menu

_____   _____

Vegetable and choice of potato included.

Grilled chicken------------$7.49
Sirloin steak --------------$15.95
Roast lamb----------------$15.89

_____   _____

Baked potato-------------$2.50
Vegetable of the day----$2.00
Rice---------------------------$1.25

_____

Soda; Mineral water------$1.19
Coffee; Tea ------------------$2.00
Milkshake--------------------$2.75

_____

Chocolate cake-------------$5.25
Ice cream---------------------$2.75
Cheesecake------------------$4.75

B. Number the conversation in the correct order.

_____ **Server:**   What do you want to drink?

_____ **Customer:**   That's all, thank you.

_____ **Customer:**   Yes, I'll have the steak and a baked potato, please.

_____ **Customer:**   Mineral water, please.

_____ **Server:**   Can I take your order?

_____ **Server:**   Anything else?

C. Make more conversations with food from the menu in Exercise A.

D. Write *How much* or *How many*.

1. _____ oranges do we need?

2. _____ tomatoes do we need?

3. _____ milk do we need?

4. _____ gallons of milk do we need?

5. _____ bread do we need?

6. _____ ice cream do we need?

E. Draw a line from the picture to the correct word. Write the name of the food under the picture.

jar

_____   _____

carton

loaf

can

_____   _____

gallon

bottle

_____   _____

box

pound

_____   _____

F. **Read the recipe. Underline the verbs in the instructions.**

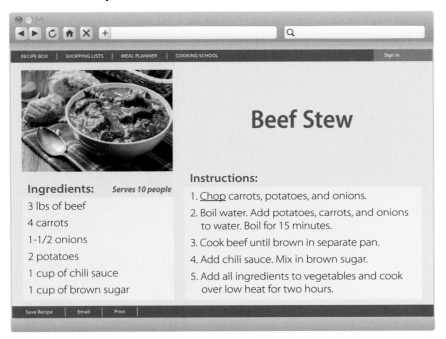

Beef Stew

Ingredients: *Serves 10 people*

3 lbs of beef
4 carrots
1-1/2 onions
2 potatoes
1 cup of chili sauce
1 cup of brown sugar

Instructions:

1. Chop carrots, potatoes, and onions.
2. Boil water. Add potatoes, carrots, and onions to water. Boil for 15 minutes.
3. Cook beef until brown in separate pan.
4. Add chili sauce. Mix in brown sugar.
5. Add all ingredients to vegetables and cook over low heat for two hours.

G. **Answer the questions about the recipe.**

1. What is the recipe for? _____

2. How many people does the recipe serve? _____

3. Write three important ingredients. _____

H. **Write the section in the supermarket and the food group for each food below.**

Food	Section	Food group
canned green beans	Canned Goods	vegetables
loaf of bread		
onions		
ground beef		
milk		
eggs		

TEAM PROJECT ✓ Plan a menu

In this project, you will plan a family menu. You are a family of four or five people. You have $150 to spend on food for the next week. What can you make for breakfast, lunch, and dinner? Make a menu and go shopping.

1. **COLLABORATE** Form a team of four or five students. In your team, you need:

Position	Job description	Student name
Student 1: **Team Leader**	Check that everyone speaks English. Check that everyone participates.	
Student 2: **Chef**	Plan meals for the family with help from the team.	
Student 3: **Shopper**	Write a shopping list for the family with help from the team.	
Students 4/5: **Spokespeople**	Prepare a class presentation with help from the team.	

2. Choose a name for your family.

3. Fill in a calendar with your meal plans for breakfast, lunch, and dinner for one week.

4. Make a shopping list. How much of each item do you need? Estimate the prices of the items on your list. Make sure the total is under $150.

5. Write a recipe for one of your meals.

6. Make a family presentation to the class. Tell the class about the meals on your menu. How much money will you spend? How much money will be left? What can you do with the money that will be left over?

Meal planning is very important. Eating leftover food for lunch the following day can help save money.

EXPLORER BARTON SEAVER

Eating Responsibly

"I'm not trying to save the fish. I'm trying to save dinner."
—Barton Seaver

A. PREDICT Look at the photo and read the quote. Answer the questions.

1. What is Barton Seaver's job?

2. What do you think is important to him?

B. PRIORITIZE Rank the items in the list below 1–5. *1* is the most important in your life and *5* is the least.

_____ food and water

_____ a place to live

_____ movies

_____ cars

_____ a job

C. Read about Barton Seaver.

Paragraph 1:   Barton Seaver is a chef and a conservationist who loves to travel. He has cooked in cities all over the world. He thinks it's important to think about where our food comes from. He also thinks it's important to produce and use food in ways that are responsible.

Paragraph 2:   After he finished studying, Barton worked in a small family restaurant in Spain. Then, he went to Morocco and traveled to a small town called Essaouria. In Essaouria, Barton went fishing with local people. People in Essaouria fish *to put food on the table*. This experience made Barton think about the food we eat and the impact it has on the environment.

Paragraph 3:   After Morocco, Barton started to talk a lot about sustainability. To be sustainable means to not run out of resources. For example, if a tree is cut down, plant another one. Barton believes that if we eat one fish, another one should be born. He believes we need to be responsible with the food we eat.

D. ANALYZE Each paragraph has a different main idea. Write the number of the paragraph.

Paragraph number	Main idea
	sustainability
	about Barton Seaver
	Barton Seaver's history

E. ANALYZE Answer the questions about the article.

1. What is Barton Seaver's job?

_____

2. What is Essaouria?

_____

3. What do you think *put food on the table* means. Talk to a partner and share your idea with the class.

_____

Housing

New apps let customers
see what furniture looks
like in their homes
before they buy it.

UNIT OUTCOMES

- Describe housing
- Interpret classified ads
- Complete a rental application
- Identify rooms and furniture
- Make a family budget

Look at the photo and answer the questions.

1. What furniture can you see?

2. Which room of a house is the furniture in?

LESSON ① Looking for a place to live

GOAL ■ Describe housing

A. Look at the picture. What are Kyung and his family reading?

B. PREDICT Work in groups. Read the questions and predict possible answers.

1. Where is Kyung from?

_____

2. Where does he work?

_____

3. Where is he living now?

_____

4. What does he need to do?

_____

C. Read and listen to the story. Then, answer the questions in Exercise B.

CD 1
TR 44

My name is Kyung. My family and I moved from Korea to Arcadia, Florida last month.
I have a good job here in Arcadia, but we need to find a place to live. We are living with
friends right now in a small house. We need to find a house, apartment, condominium, or
mobile home. We need to buy furniture and open a bank account, too. We have a lot to do.

D. **INTERPRET** Scan the housing advertisements and look at the pictures. Write the correct number next to each picture.

1. FOR RENT

Three-bedroom house
Rent: $1,200 a month
Address: 315 Madison St.

Contact Agent

2. MOBILE HOME

Three-bedroom mobile home
Rent: $750 a month
Address: 1700 Grove St.

Contact Agent

3. FOR RENT

Three-bedroom apartment
Rent: $700 a month
Address: 200 Atlantic Ave. #211

Contact Agent

4. CONDO

Three-bedroom condominium
For sale: $85,000
Address: 12 Shady Glen

Contact Agent

a.

_____

b.

_____

c.

_____

d.
_____

E. Study the chart with your classmates and teacher.

Information question	Answer
How **much** is the **house**?	It's $1,200 a month.
What **kind** of **hous**ing is **Num**ber **2**?	It's a mobile home.
Where is the condo**min**ium?	It's on Shady Glen.
How many **bed**rooms does the **a**part**ment have**?	It has three bedrooms.

STRESS AND RHYTHM

Emphasize the bold syllables in the chart and say the others quickly.

F. Ask a partner information questions about the advertisements in Exercise D.

G. Read about Rosa and Gilberto. Then, ask and answer questions with a partner.

Rosa
I live in a condominium.
It has three bedrooms.
It's on Adams Street.
I like my home.

Gilberto
I live in an apartment.
It has one bedroom.
It's on Butcher Street.
I don't like my home. I want to move.

H. SURVEY Do a housing survey in your class. Ask every classmate.

What kind of home do you live in?	Number of classmates
House	
Condominium	
Apartment	
Mobile home	
Other	

I. CREATE Make a pie chart of your survey. Use the example to help you.

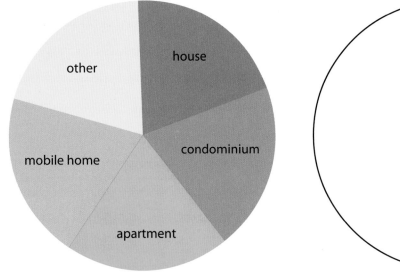

LESSON **2** Finding a home

GOAL ▊ Interpret classified ads

A. SURVEY Talk in groups about your home.

1. What kind of home do you live in?

2. How many bedrooms does it have?

3. Is your home large or small?

4. Is your home one story or two story?

5. Do you have a yard or a balcony?

6. Is your home old or new?

B. Listen to the descriptions and point to the correct house.

CD 1
TR 45–48

a.

b.

Balcony

c.

d.

C. Match the pictures with the descriptions below.

_____ 1. This large four-bedroom, three-bathroom house is the perfect rental for big families. The house is old but is in very good condition. The neighborhood is quiet and comfortable. There is a beautiful view from the balcony. This two-story house rents for $2,500 a month, and utilities are included.

_____ 2. Come and see this new, small, one-story dream house. It is in a small and friendly neighborhood. This house rents for $1,800 a month. It has one bedroom, one bathroom, and a large kitchen. You will love it when you see it!

_____ 3. Sometimes older is better. This small two-bedroom, one-bathroom house has an interesting history. The same person has owned it for 50 years. Rent it for an amazing $1,500 a month.

_____ 4. If you want to rent a big home and money is not important, rent this very large five-bedroom, three-bathroom house with a swimming pool. It is a great value for $3,000 a month.

D. CLASSIFY Complete the table with information from Exercise C. Then, ask a partner about the houses.

EXAMPLES: Which house has a pool?
Which house has two bedrooms?

	House #1	House #2	House #3	House #4
Bedrooms				
Bathrooms				
Monthly rent				
Amenities				

E. INTERPRET Scan the classified ads for the houses in Exercise C. Which ad is for which house? Write the number of the house.

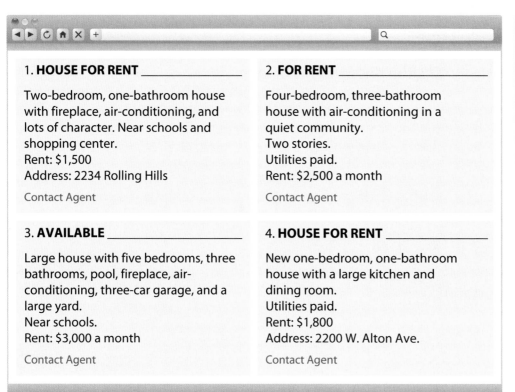

1. HOUSE FOR RENT _____

Two-bedroom, one-bathroom house with fireplace, air-conditioning, and lots of character. Near schools and shopping center.
Rent: $1,500
Address: 2234 Rolling Hills

Contact Agent

2. FOR RENT _____

Four-bedroom, three-bathroom house with air-conditioning in a quiet community.
Two stories.
Utilities paid.
Rent: $2,500 a month

Contact Agent

3. AVAILABLE _____

Large house with five bedrooms, three bathrooms, pool, fireplace, air-conditioning, three-car garage, and a large yard.
Near schools.
Rent: $3,000 a month

Contact Agent

4. HOUSE FOR RENT _____

New one-bedroom, one-bathroom house with a large kitchen and dining room.
Utilities paid.
Rent: $1,800
Address: 2200 W. Alton Ave.

Contact Agent

AMENITIES

Amenities are extras a home has to improve value. For example: balcony, large kitchen, large backyard, or a swimming pool.

F. **Look at the ads and ask a partner the questions below.**

RENTALS

1. FOR RENT	2. FOR RENT	3. FOR RENT
Two-bedroom, two-bathroom condo. Utilities paid and air-conditioning included. Near parks and schools. Dallas City **$1,000** Ask inside for more information	Four-bedroom, three-bathroom house with a pool, fireplace, and balcony. 5253 Bountiful Street, Luxury Heights **$1,400** Ask inside for more information	Clean, three-bedroom apartment with air-conditioning. Refrigerator included. No pets. **$1,200** Ask inside for more information
4. FOR RENT	**5. FOR RENT**	**6. FOR RENT**
One-bedroom, one-bathroom apartment. New carpets. Sycamore St., Costa Mesa **$900** Ask inside for more information	Three-bedroom, one-bathroom condo with air-conditioning. Water paid. Bridgemont **$1,400** Ask inside for more information	Like-new two-bedroom mobile home. Utilities paid. Seawall Estates, Newton **$1,100** Ask inside for more information

1. Which home is under $1,000 a month?

2. Which homes have air-conditioning?

3. Which home has a refrigerator included?

4. Which home has three bathrooms?

G. **CREATE** **In a group, write a classified ad. Answer these questions in your ad.**

1. How much is the rent?

2. How many bedrooms are there?

3. How many bathrooms are there?

4. What amenities are there?

5. Who do you call?

6. What's the phone number?

H. **APPLY** **Look on the Internet to find classified ads for your area. Find a home for yourself. Report to the class.**

LESSON **3** At the rental agency

GOAL ■ Complete a rental application

A. PREDICT Look at the picture. Where is Kyung? What is he doing?

B. CLASSIFY Listen to the conversation. What does Kyung need? What does he want? Complete the table.

Needs	Wants
three-bedroom house	

C. Look at the ads and choose the best home for Kyung. Work in groups.

1. FOR RENT

Two-bedroom, two-bathroom house with a big yard.
Utilities paid.
Near schools.

Rent: $1,050 a month
Contact Agent

2. FOR RENT

Three-bedroom, two-bathroom apartment with a big living room, a small yard, and a separate garage. Utilities paid. No deposit.

Rent: $750 a month
Contact Agent

3. FOR RENT

Three-bedroom, two-story house with garage.
Air-conditioning.
Near schools and shopping.
Rent: $1,500 a month
Contact Agent

4. FOR RENT

Four-bedroom, three-bathroom, one-story condo with a big yard.
No pets.

Rent: $925 a month
Contact Agent

D. INTERPRET Discuss the rental application with your classmates and teacher.

RENTAL APPLICATION FORM

Applicant: __Kyung Kim__   Interviewed by: __Paula Wharton__

Present Address: __33457 Akron Street, Arcadia, FL 34265__

Phone: __555-5059__

Prior Address: __134-2 Jongun-Dong, Jongno-Gu, Seoul, South Korea__

Social Security Number: __123-45-6789__   E-mail Address: __kkim@ma1l.com__

Landlord: __Fred Wharton__   Prior Landlord: __N/A__

Employer: __Shift Manufacturing__   Position: __Computer Technician__

Personal References: __James Baker; Manuel Acevedo__   Relationship: __Boss; Supervisor__

Co-Applicant or Spouse: __Anh Kim__

Employer: __Rosco Metals__   Position: __Assembly Worker__

Personal Reference: __George Pratt__   Relationship: __Supervisor__

E. Answer the questions about the application.

1. What's Kyung's present address?

_____

2. What was his address before he came to Florida?

_____

3. What is the name of the company where he works?

_____

4. What is the name of the company where Anh works?

_____

5. Who are Kyung's references?

_____

F. Study the questions with your classmates and teacher.

Information Questions		
What is your name?	**Where** did you live before?	**Who** is your employer?
Where do you live now?	**How** long did you live there?	**What** is your position?

G. Look at the rental application in Exercise D. Practice asking a partner questions. Your partner is Kyung.

H. Interview your partner and complete the application for them.

RENTAL APPLICATION FORM

Applicant: _____ Interviewed by: _____

Present Address: _____

Phone: _____

Prior Address: _____

Social Security Number: _____ E-mail Address: _____

Landlord: _____ Prior Landlord: _____

Employer: _____ Position: _____

Personal References: _____ Relationship: _____

Co-Applicant or Spouse: _____

Employer: _____ Position: _____

Personal Reference: _____ Relationship: _____

I. **APPLY** Look online and find a rental application. Share it with the class.

LESSON **4** We need furniture!

A. **INTERPRET** Read about the home Kyung is going to rent. How many bedrooms and bathrooms does it have? How much is the rent? What is nearby?

FOR RENT

Three-bedroom, two-bathroom house with a big living room, a separate garage, a new remodeled kitchen, a new washer/dryer, dishwasher, stove, and oven.
Utilities paid and no deposit required.
Rent: **$1,200** a month

Ask inside for more information

CD 1
TR 50–53

B. Listen to the descriptions. Circle the description of Kyung's new home.

Home 1   Home 2   Home 3   Home 4

C. Complete the floor plan key with words from the box.

bathroom
~~bedroom~~
kitchen
yard
living room
dining room

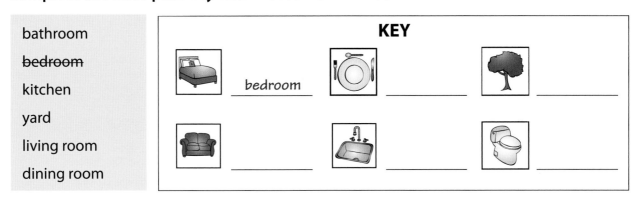

KEY

bedroom   _____   _____

_____   _____   _____

D. Look at the floor plans. Which one is Kyung's new home?

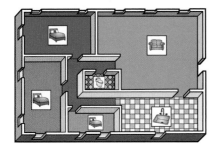 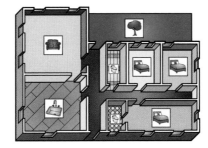 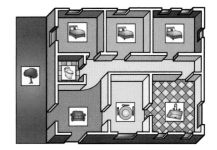

E. Write the new words under each piece of furniture.

armchair	coffee table	dresser	end table
bookcase	couch	dining room table	table lamp

$850.89	$34.49	$369.89	$449.99

$875.00	$225.89	$275.99	$149.99

F. **PLAN** Where would you put the furniture in Exercise E? Draw on the floor plan.

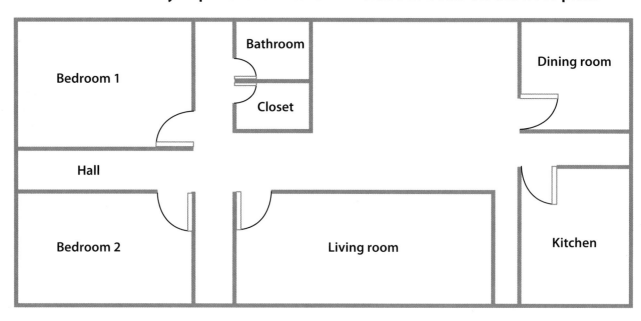

G. Study the photo with your classmates and teacher.

The picture is over the couch.

The lamp is on the end table.

The fireplace is between the armchairs.

The couch is behind the coffee table.

The coffee table is in front of the couch.

The couch is next to the end table.

The coffee table is in the living room.

The end table is in the corner.

H. Practice the conversation with a partner. Make similar conversations using the furniture and floor plan in exercises E and F.

Student A: Where is the end table?

Student B: It's in the living room next to the couch.

I. CALCULATE Decide what you want to buy and complete the invoice. Look at Exercise E for the prices.

McCarthy's Furniture Warehouse			
Quantity	Merchandise	Unit price	Total
1	couch	$850.89	$850.89
	armchair		
	end table		
	coffee table		
	table lamp		
	dining room table		
	dresser		
		Total	

LESSON ⑤ Family budget

GOAL ▪ Make a family budget

A. **PREDICT** Look at the picture. What are Kyung and his wife doing?

B. **INTERPRET** Read about managing money and budgets. Underline any new words.

Be careful with your money. Follow these steps:

- Deposit your paycheck in the bank.
- Keep cash for emergencies.
- Only withdraw money from the bank when it is part of your budget.
- Don't use credit cards a lot. Use an ATM when you need cash.

Plan your budget. Follow these steps:

- Write down how much you need every month for rent, food, gas, water, and electricity.
- Write down how much you need to buy other things, like clothes.
- Plan how much money you need every month for entertainment.
- Plan how much you can put in your savings account for emergencies and for the future.

C. Match each word with a definition. Write the correct number.

| 1. budget | 2. ATM | 3. paycheck | 4. deposit | 5. withdraw | 6. cash |

_____ a. put money in the bank   _____ b. paper money and coins

_____ c. a plan for your money   _____ d. automated teller machine

_____ e. take money out of the bank   _____ f. check received for work

D. Study Kyung and Anh's family budget with your classmates and teacher.

Monthly Income	
Kyung's wages	$3,000
Anh's wages	$2,500
Total Income	
Monthly Expenses	
Rent	$1,200
Gas	
Electric	$125
Water	$32
Food	
Life insurance	$91
Auto insurance	$125
Gasoline	
Phone	
Credit cards	$300
Entertainment	
Clothing	$200
Household repairs	
Savings	$100
Taxes	$900
Total Expenses	

🎧 **E. CALCULATE** Listen and complete the budget.
Then, calculate the totals.

CD 1
TR 54

F. Study the chart with your classmates and teacher.

> **WAGE AND SALARY**
> wage = amount of money based on hours worked
> salary = fixed amount paid each year

Modals: *May* and *Might*			
Subject	**Modal**	**Base verb**	**Example sentence**
I, You, He, She, We, They	might	spend	We **might** spend $300 a month on food.

G. **Practice the conversation with a partner. Make new conversations using the information from the budget in Exercise D.**

Student A (Anh):   How much do we spend on water every month?

Student B (Kyung):   We spend about $32.

H. **PLAN** **Work with a partner. Imagine that you are a family. Make a budget. Write the information below.**

Student A: How much do you think we spend on clothing each month?

Student B: We might spend $200.

Monthly Income	
_____	_____
_____	_____
Total Income	_____
Monthly Expenses	
_____	_____
_____	_____
_____	_____
_____	_____
_____	_____
_____	_____
_____	_____
_____	_____
_____	_____
_____	_____
_____	_____
_____	_____
_____	_____
Total Expenses	_____

Before You Watch

A. Look at the picture and answer the questions.

1. Where is the Sanchez family?

2. What are they doing?

While You Watch

B. Watch the video. Read the statements and write *T* for true and *F* for false.

1. Hector wants something to eat. _____

2. Mr. and Mrs. Sanchez are making a family budget. _____

3. The coffee maker breaks when Hector tries to use it. _____

4. Mr. Sanchez hopes to save money on another item so he can buy a new microwave. _____

5. Hector wants to go out for lunch. _____

6. Hector and his parents go shopping for a coffee maker. _____

Check Your Understanding

C. Circle the words in parentheses to complete each sentence.

1. Why do people make (expenses / budgets)?

2. A budget keeps track of how much money people (spend / add) in relation to how much they earn.

3. Many people make budgets to keep track of monthly (expenses / plans).

4. If you know which items you spend money on each month, you can make smart choices to (save / earn) money.

5. For example, you may choose to cook more and eat out less if you (plan / spend) to buy an expensive item next month.

Review

A. Complete the questions.

1. _____ kind of housing do you want?

2. _____ is the rent?

3. _____ house do you want, the three- or four-bedroom?

4. _____ is the condominium? Is it on Main Street?

5. _____ bedrooms does the apartment have?

B. Scan the classified ads and answer the questions below.

1. FOR RENT

Three-bedroom, two-bathroom condo with fireplace and air-conditioning.
Near schools and park.
Utilities paid.
Rent: $1,200
Contact Agent

2. FOR RENT

Two-bedroom, two-bathroom with a fireplace, air-conditioning, a large garage, and a balcony.
Near local parks.

Rent: $900 a month
Contact Agent

3. AVAILABLE

Large five-bedroom, three-bathroom house with a pool.
Near schools.
Rent: $2,900 a month
Contact Agent

4. HOUSE FOR RENT

Two-bedroom, one-bathroom mobile home on a spacious lot.
Utilities paid.
Rent: $700
Contact Agent

1. Which homes have a fireplace? _____

2. Which homes have utilities included? _____

3. Which home is less than $900? _____

4. Which homes have air-conditioning? _____

5. Which homes are near schools? _____

C. Answer the questions.

1. What is your present address? _____

2. What is your prior address? _____

3. What is your employer's name? _____

4. How many children live in your house? _____

5. Give one reference. _____

D. Write sentences about the location of furniture in the picture. Use prepositions.

1. _The fireplace is under the picture._ _____

2. _____

3. _____

4. _____

5. _____

Learner Log

I can complete a rental application.   I can make a family budget.
☐ Yes ☐ No ☐ Maybe   ☐ Yes ☐ No ☐ Maybe

E. Look at the rental application. Where do you write the following information? Circle the correct answers.

RENTAL APPLICATION

Date: **1.** _____   Name: **2.** _____

Present Address: **3.** _____

Prior Address: **4.** _____

Employer: **5.** _____

Position: **6.** _____

How many adults in unit: **7.** _____

How many children in unit: **8.** _____

1. June 3rd

   a. 1   b. 2   c. 5   d. 6

2. 8237 Henderson Park Rd.

   a. 2   b. 6   c. 4   d. 5

3. Sift Company

   a. 1   b. 3   c. 5   d. 6

F. Look at the budget and write the answers.

Monthly Income	
Kyung's wages	_____ $3,000
Anh's wages	_____ $2,500
Total Income	_____
Monthly Expenses	
Rent	_____ $1,200
Gas	_____ $50
Electric	_____ $125
Water	_____ $32
Food	_____ $1,100
Life insurance	_____ $91
Auto insurance	_____ $125
Total Expenses	_____

1. What is Kyung's income?

   _____

2. How much is the apartment?

   _____

3. How much are the utilities?

   _____

4. What is the total income?

   _____

5. What are the total expenses?

   _____

TEAM PROJECT ✓ Plan a move

Your team is a family who is going to move to a new home. Work together to plan the move.

1. **COLLABORATE** Form a team of four or five students. In your team, you need:

Position	Job description	Student name
Student 1: **Team Leader**	Check that everyone speaks English. Check that everyone participates.	
Student 2: **Finance Planner**	Make a family budget with help from the team. Plan to pay rent and buy furniture.	
Student 3: **Writer**	Write a classified ad and fill out a rental application with help from the team.	
Students 4/5: **Decorators**	Buy and arrange furniture in the home with help from the team.	

2. Describe your family and the home you want. Write a classified ad for the home you want.

   • How many bedrooms do you need?

   • What kind of home do you need (house, condo, apartment)?

   • How much money can you pay for rent?

3. Fill out a rental application.

4. Make a family budget.

5. Make a list of the furniture you need and fill out an invoice for furniture.

6. Make a floor plan of the home and add the furniture.

7. Report to the class. Show the floor plan and classified ad.

EXPLORER GORDON WILTSIE

Blending In

"Asking permission is often deadly for spontaneity, but works beautifully if you can spend enough time together that your subject can relax."
—Gordon Wiltsie

A. **PREDICT** Draw a line from the word or phrase to the definition. Guess first and then use a dictionary.

vanish	to take a picture
culture	to disappear
pose	to be part of something
take a shot	way of life
blend in	to get ready for a photograph

B. **Read the interview with Gordon Wiltsie.**

Interviewer: Gordon, what are your favorite subjects? In other words, what kind of photos do you take?

Wiltsie: I'm very interested in vanishing cultures.

Interviewer: Vanishing?

Wiltsie: Yes, I mean cultures that most people don't know a lot about and may not be here in 50 years.

Interviewer: How do you get pictures of people that are so natural?

Wiltsie: I live with them and work with them. I try to be part of their culture. I do chores and help where I can. I try to understand them. Then, when they are comfortable and trust me, I wait for the shot and take it.

Interviewer: I see. **So just to be clear, you don't ask people to pose for photos. Is that right?**

Wiltsie: That's right. I don't ask them to pose for photos. I take photos of what they do every day. I take photos of people in their homes, or in nature. I take photos of people talking to each other, working, or playing. I just try to blend in.

Interviewer: What do you mean, blend in?

Wiltsie: I try to be part of their community. I don't want to be a stranger or someone from the outside.

Interviewer: Very interesting. Thank you.

C. **ANALYZE** **Look at the clarifications in bold in the interview. Write them under the clarification strategy below.**

1. Ask directly.

_____

2. Repeat a word like a question for clarification.

_____

3. Repeat an idea in the interviewer's own words.

_____

D. **APPLY** **Ask and answer the questions with a partner. Add two more. Use clarification strategies when necessary.**

What is your name?   What do you like to do?

Where do you live?   Where did you live before?

The Food Waste Rebel

Tristram Stuart arranges food at a Feeding the 5000 event.

In Unit 3, you met chef and conservationist Barton Seaver. Barton wants people to be responsible for the food they eat so that it doesn't run out. You will now meet someone else who wants people to take responsibility for the food they eat, but more importantly, to stop wasting it.

Before You Watch

A. Read the sentences. Match each word in bold with the correct definition below by writing the sentence numbers.

1. All the food that customers don't eat is **waste**. The restaurant throws it away.

2. These large boxes from the **plant** contain fresh fruit and vegetables.

3. If the tomatoes are damaged, the supermarket throws them in the **dumpster**.

4. In some countries, food is a **scarcity**. Many people don't have enough to eat.

5. Food is **valuable**. Everyone in the world needs it to live.

_____ something left over; unwanted

_____ a large trash container

_____ very small amount; shortage

_____ factory; building where something is made

_____ something worth a lot; very important

B. You are going to watch a video. What do you think it will be about? Look at the pictures and circle one or more of the topics below. Share your predictions with a partner.

feeding animals	shopping for clothes	housing	school
supermarkets	cooking	weather	family
classified ads	calendars and schedules	saving food	furniture

C. What does the information in Exercises A and B tell you about the video you will watch? Discuss as a class.

While You Watch

A. **Read each question. Watch and listen for the information and circle the correct answers.**

1. Does Tristram Stuart have black hair?

   a. Yes, he does.   b. No, he doesn't.

2. Do the workers at the food plant in Kenya have blond hair?

   a. Yes, they do.   b. No, they don't.

3. Are the people at the free feast the same age?

   a. Yes, they are.   b. No, they aren't.

4. Do the pigs have white stripes?

   a. Yes, they do.   b. No, they don't.

5. Do the pigs eat green vegetables?

   a. Yes, they do.   b. No, they don't.

6. Does Tristram say he is from Canada?

   a. Yes, he does.   b. No, he doesn't.

B. **Watch the video again. Write a short summary about what you learned and discuss with a partner.**

_____

_____

_____

_____

_____

_____

_____

C. **Look at your predictions on page 109. Are your predictions about the video correct? Discuss with the class.**

After You Watch

WORD FOCUS

A *catastrophe* is something that causes great damage or harm; a disaster.

A. What kind of catastrophe does Tristram Stuart want to prevent? Look at each picture and caption below. Check (✓) the correct answer.

flooding ☐   hunger ☐   forest fires ☐   drought ☐

B. Read the sentences and circle *True* or *False*. Correct the false sentences in your notebook.

1. If food looks bad, supermarkets sometimes throw it in the dumpster.   True   False
2. Half of the world's food supply is wasted.   True   False
3. Feedback is an organization that helps people build farms.   True   False
4. There are millions of hungry people in the country of Kenya.   True   False
5. Pigs have no problems eating food from supermarket dumpsters.   True   False

C. Why do we waste food? Think about the food you throw away and give a reason.

EXAMPLE   *We cook or make too much.*

_____

D. What can you do to reduce food waste in your own home? Read the list and check (✓) the idea(s) you agree with. Add to your own ideas and be prepared to discuss in small groups.

__ Buy less
__ Prepare smaller amounts
__ Eat only one or two times a day
__ Share food with family, friends, and neighbors
__ Keep food longer than the dates on the package
__ Put food in the refrigerator to keep it fresh

_____
_____
_____

Our Community

There's always something to do in Times Square—even when it's raining.

UNIT OUTCOMES

☐ Describe your community

☐ Scan an Internet search page

☐ Give and follow directions

☐ Read a message or letter

☐ Write and send a letter

Look at the photo and answer the questions.

1. What places can people visit in the city?

2. What ways can people find things to do in a city?

GOAL ▪ Describe your community

A. INTERPRET Read the Palm City web page.

◀ ▶ C 🏠 ✕ +   🔍

WELCOME TO PALM CITY   ▶ SITEMAP   ▶ FIND US   ▶ E-MAIL

| HOME | ABOUT | EVENTS | DIRECTORY | PHOTOS | CONTACT US |

UPCOMING EVENTS:

02.10 - Urban Street Festival

02.17 - Gathering in the Park

02.24 - Sports Day

03.03 - Outdoor Theater

03.14 - Farmer's Market

03.21 - Gathering in the Park

Our small, planned community is perfect for family life. Beautiful homes and schools are in the northwest. The Palm City Mall has over 100 stores and is in the northeast. Spend your weekends at Valley Entertainment Center in the southeast. There is a bowling alley, a movie theater, a miniature golf course, and much more. The industrial area has factories and other businesses and is in the southwest part of town. We have planned it so the bus circles our town in exactly one hour.

Newcomers

Calendar

More

B. Fill in the chart about Palm City.

North

West

1.

northwest

homes and schools

3.

2.

4.

East

South

C. **ANALYZE** Look at the bus schedule. Write the names of the streets on the map.

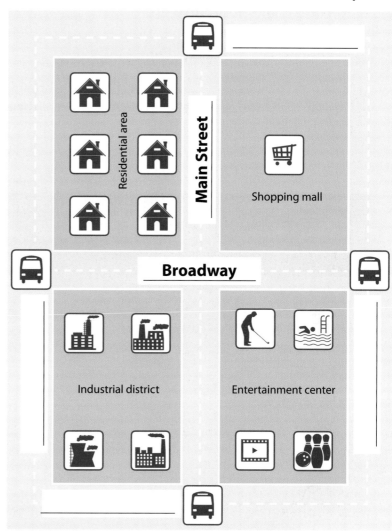

Information Questions			
Question word		**Subject**	**Base verb**
When	does	the bus	stop	in the residential area?
Where				

D. **Practice the conversations. Use the information in Exercise C to make new conversations.**

Student A: When does the bus stop in the <u>residential area</u>?
Student B: It stops at <u>7:00 a.m.</u>

Student B: Where does the bus stop at <u>8:45</u>?
Student A: It stops in <u>the industrial district.</u>

E. CLASSIFY Read the words in the box and write them in the correct columns. Then, listen and check your answers.

CD 2
TR 1

apartment	courthouse	hardware store	pharmacy
bank	department store	hospital	police station
city hall	fast-food restaurant	~~house~~	post office
clothes store	fire station	library	shoe store
condominium	gas station	mobile home	supermarket

Residential	Public and Service	Retail

_____house_____ _____ _____

_____ _____ _____

_____ _____ _____

_____ _____ _____

_____ _____

_____ _____

_____ _____

_____ _____

F. List places in your community that are close to your home.

_____ _____ _____

_____ _____ _____

_____ _____ _____

_____ _____ _____

LESSON ② What's the number?

GOAL ▮ Scan an Internet search page

A. PREDICT Look at the picture of Marie. What is she doing?

B. Read the paragraph about Marie.

> Marie lives in Palm City. She is a nurse at the hospital. She wants to send a package to her friend in Brazil. She is searching online for the telephone number and address of the nearest post office because she has questions: Does she send the package with insurance? Does she send it first-class? When will the package arrive in Brazil?

C. Circle the correct answer.

1. Why is Marie doing an online search?
   a. She wants to send a letter.
   b. She needs information.
   c. She has a friend in Brazil.

2. What does Marie want to do?
   a. She wants to get insurance.
   b. She wants to travel to Brazil.
   c. She wants to send a package.

D. INTERPRET Scan the Palm City Directory. Circle any words you don't know.

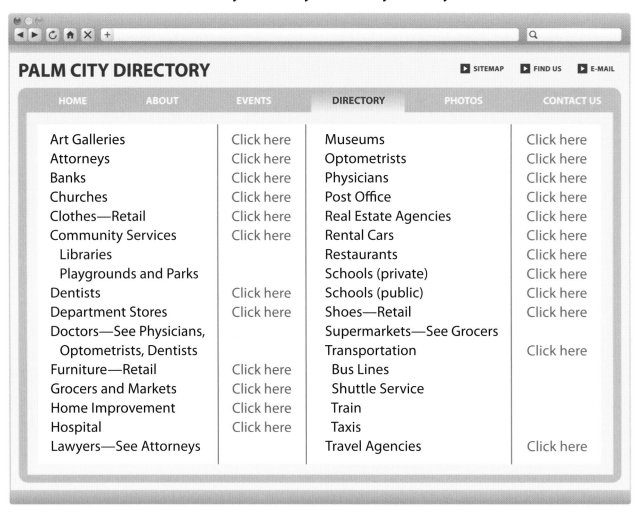

E. INTERPRET Write the links that will help Marie find locations in Palm City. Complete the table.

Marie needs ...	Link
to send a package.	Post Office
to buy food.	
a new sweater.	
a taxi to the airport.	
to find a place to go for dinner.	
to repair a broken window.	
to see a lawyer.	

Simple Present	
Subject	**Verb**
I, You, We, They	need, want
He, She	needs, wants

F. INTERPRET Study the directory with your classmates and teacher.

Palm City Government Agencies and Services

City Hall 160 W. Broadway	555-3300	**Angel Park** 137 Monroe St.	555-3224
Courthouse 150 W. Broadway	555-5245	**Lilly Community Park** 275 Carpenter	555-2211
DMV (Department of Motor Vehicles) 375 Western Ave. Information Appointments	 555-2227 555-2778	**Police Department** **Emergencies call 911** 140 W. Broadway	555-4867
Fire Department **Emergencies call 911** 145 W. Broadway	555-3473	**Schools (Public)** **Jefferson Middle** 122 Jefferson St.	555-2665
Library (Public) 125 E. Broadway	555-7323	**Lincoln High** 278 Lincoln Ave.	555-8336
Playgrounds and Parks **Department of Parks and Recreation** 160 W. Broadway Suite 15	 555-7275	**Washington Elementary** 210 Washington St.	555-5437
		U.S. Post Office 151 E. Broadway	555-6245

G. CD 2 TR 2 **Listen and practice the conversation. Then, ask a partner for information about the** *post office, courthouse, DMV, fire department, City Hall,* **and** *Jefferson Middle School.*

Student A: Where's the post office?
Student B: It's at 151 East Broadway.
Student A: What's the phone number?
Student B: It's 555-6245.

H. CD 2 TR 3–7 **CLASSIFY** Cover the directory and listen to the conversations. Write the places, addresses, and phone numbers you hear in the table.

Place	Address	Phone
1.		
2.		
3.		
4.		
5.		

I. APPLY What are the most important phone numbers to have? Make a list with a group.

LESSON ③ Finding your way

GOAL ▢ Give and follow directions

A. INTERPRET Look at the map and practice the conversation. Make new conversations with other places on the map.

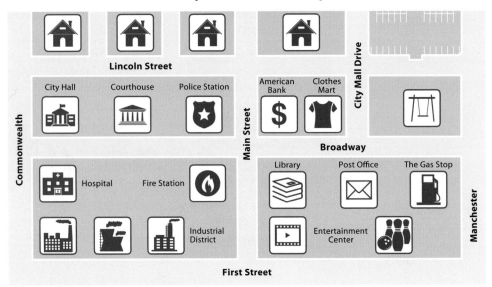

Student A: Where is the bank?
Student B: It's on Broadway.

B. Study the prepositions with your classmates and teacher.

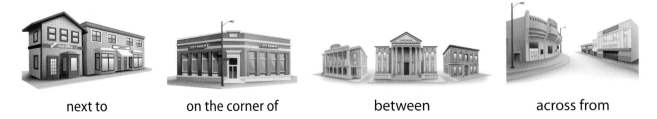

next to   on the corner of   between   across from

C. Look at the map in Exercise A. Complete the sentences with prepositions.

1. The gas station is _____ Broadway and Manchester.

2. The courthouse is _____ City Hall and the police station.

3. The post office is _____ the library.

4. The police station is _____ the fire station.

5. City Hall is _____ the hospital.

6. The post office is _____ the library and the gas station.

120 Unit 5

D. Marie's friend needs directions. Listen to the conversation. Find Marie's apartment on the map.

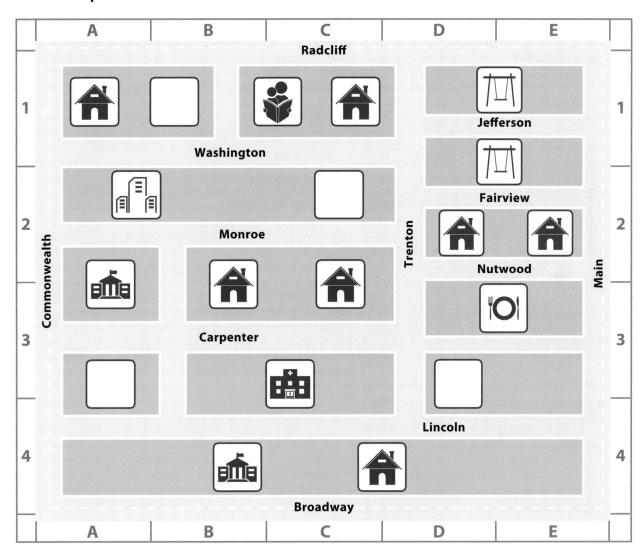

E. Listen to the directions. Find the locations on the map.

F. **IDENTIFY** Write the letter and number for each location below.

1. the museum   A3

2. the real estate office   _____

3. the computer store   _____

4. the coffee shop   _____

G. Study the chart with your classmates and teacher.

	Imperatives		
	Base verb		**Example sentence**
you	go	straight straight ahead	**Go** straight three blocks. **Go** straight ahead.
	turn	left right around	**Turn** left on Nutwood. **Turn** right on Nutwood. **Turn** around.
	stop	on the left on the right	**Stop** on the left. **Stop** on the right.

H. Study the map with your classmates and teacher.

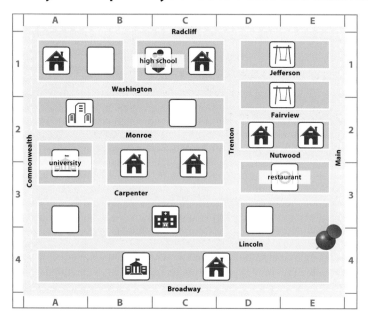

I. Look at the map above. Start at the red pin and write directions to the high school.

The high school: _Go straight ahead on Main for three blocks. Then,_ _____

_____

_____

J. On a separate piece of paper, write directions to the restaurant and the university.

K. **APPLY** On a sheet of paper, write directions from your school to your home.

GOAL ▇ Read a message or letter

A. Read Marie's e-mail to her friend Raquel in Brazil.

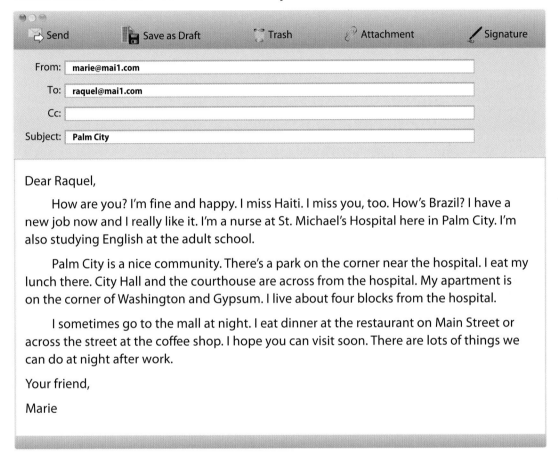

Send | Save as Draft | Trash | Attachment | Signature

From: marie@mai1.com

To: raquel@mai1.com

Cc:

Subject: Palm City

Dear Raquel,

How are you? I'm fine and happy. I miss Haiti. I miss you, too. How's Brazil? I have a new job now and I really like it. I'm a nurse at St. Michael's Hospital here in Palm City. I'm also studying English at the adult school.

Palm City is a nice community. There's a park on the corner near the hospital. I eat my lunch there. City Hall and the courthouse are across from the hospital. My apartment is on the corner of Washington and Gypsum. I live about four blocks from the hospital.

I sometimes go to the mall at night. I eat dinner at the restaurant on Main Street or across the street at the coffee shop. I hope you can visit soon. There are lots of things we can do at night after work.

Your friend,

Marie

B. Answer the questions in complete sentences. Use prepositions.

1. Where does Marie eat lunch? Where is it?

   She eats lunch in the park. It's on the corner near the hospital.

2. Where does Marie work? Where is the building?

   _____

3. Where is the courthouse?

   _____

4. Where does Marie eat dinner? Where is the building?

   _____

C. Study the charts with your classmates and teacher.

Simple Present	
Subject	**Verb**
I, You, We, They	eat
He, She, It	eats

Simple Present: *Be*		
Subject	***Be***	
I	am	happy
You, We, They	are	sad
He, She, It	is	tired

Present Continuous			
Subject	***Be***	**Base verb + *ing***	**Example sentence**
I	am	writing	I **am** (I**'m**) **writing** this letter in English.
You, We, They	are	going	We **are** (We**'re**) **going** to the mall.
He, She, It	is	eating	He **is** (He**'s**) **eating** at the coffee shop.

D. Read the e-mail from Raquel to her friend. Circle the simple present verbs. Underline the present continuous verbs.

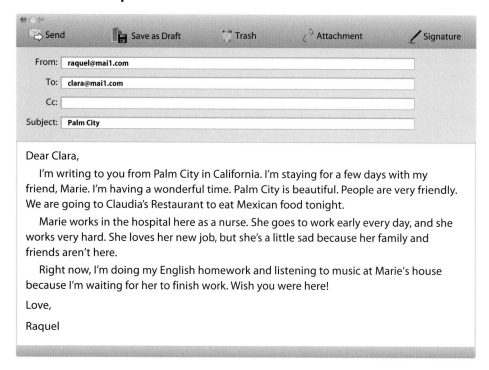

Send   Save as Draft   Trash   Attachment   Signature

From: raquel@mai1.com
To: clara@mai1.com
Cc:
Subject: Palm City

Dear Clara,

I'm writing to you from Palm City in California. I'm staying for a few days with my friend, Marie. I'm having a wonderful time. Palm City is beautiful. People are very friendly. We are going to Claudia's Restaurant to eat Mexican food tonight.

Marie works in the hospital here as a nurse. She goes to work early every day, and she works very hard. She loves her new job, but she's a little sad because her family and friends aren't here.

Right now, I'm doing my English homework and listening to music at Marie's house because I'm waiting for her to finish work. Wish you were here!

Love,

Raquel

E. INFER On a piece of paper, answer the questions in complete sentences.

1. Is Raquel happy or sad?

2. What is Raquel doing right now?

3. What does Marie do every day?

4. Is Marie happy or sad?

F. **PREDICT** Read the questions and predict the answers. Then, listen to the e-mail from Raquel to her husband, Antonio, and check your answers.

1. How is the weather in Palm City?

a. cold   b. warm   c. hot

2. What are in the parks?

a. palm trees and cactus plants   b. children   c. tables

3. Where does the bus stop?

a. near the park   b. near the shopping mall   c. near Marie's house

G. **APPLY** On a separate piece of paper, write sentences about the city where you live.

1. Where do you live? What is the name of your city?

2. Describe your city. Is it beautiful, crowded, old, new, big, or small?

3. How is the weather in your city? Is the weather cold, warm, or hot most of the time?

4. Where do you like to go in your city? Do you like to go to stores, restaurants, entertainment places, or parks?

H. **CREATE** Complete the e-mail with your sentences from Exercise G.

| Send | Save as Draft | Trash | Attachment | Signature |

From:

To:

Cc:

Subject:

Dear _____ ,

I hope you are well. I'm fine. I live in _____ . It is _____

_____

_____

_____

_____

LESSON **5** # The city is beautiful!

GOAL Write and send a letter

A. CLASSIFY Read the envelope and complete the table.

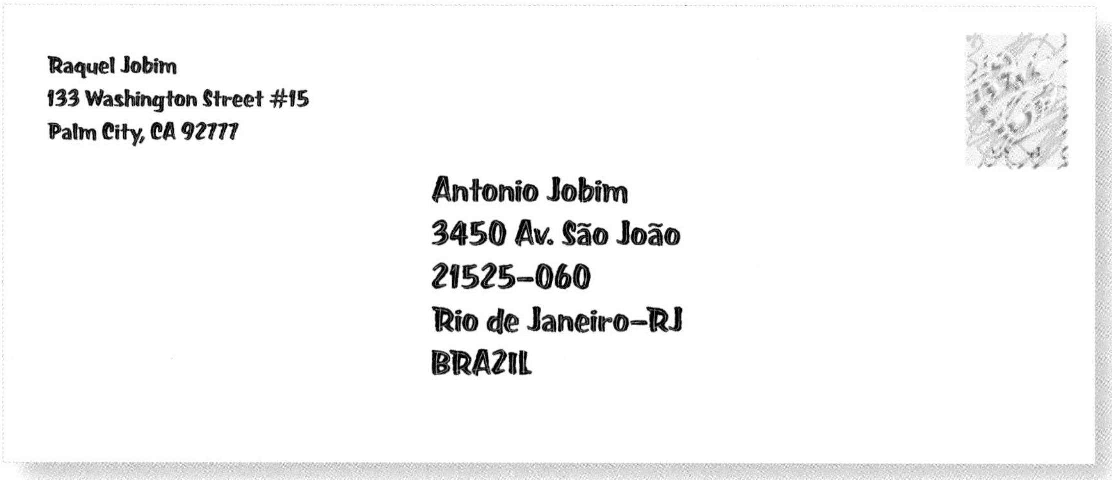
Raquel Jobim
133 Washington Street #15
Palm City, CA 92777
Antonio Jobim
3450 Av. São João
21525-060
Rio de Janeiro-RJ
BRAZIL

From:		To:	
Street:		Street:	
City:		City:	
Zip code:		Zip code:	
State:		State:	
Country:		Country:	

B. Complete the envelope from you to a partner's address.

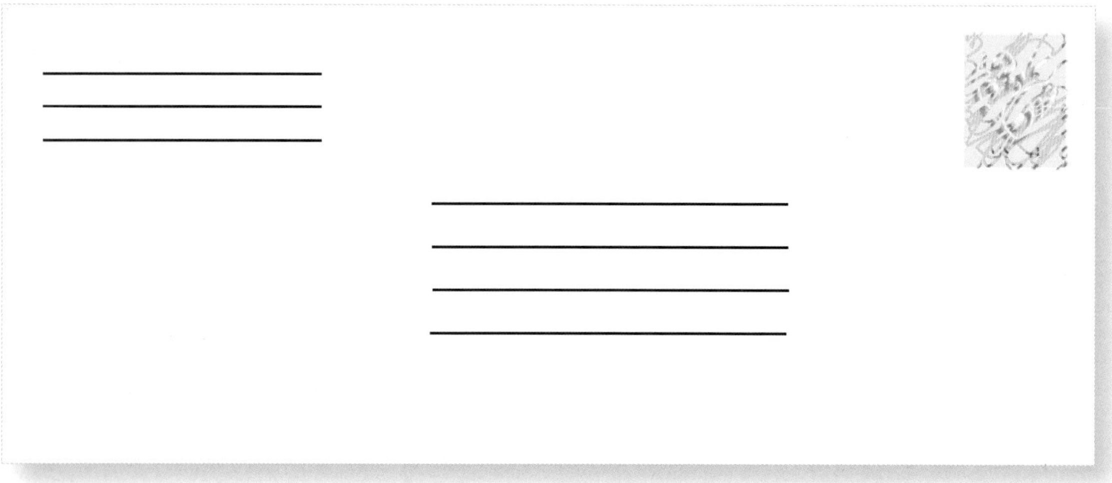

C. Study the parts of a letter. Then, listen to a lecture and number the parts.

CD 2
TR 11

Parts of a letter	Example
_____ body	most of the information
_____ closing	*Sincerely, Love, Love always, Your friend,*
_____ closing sentence	*Call me! I hope to see you soon.*
___1___ date	*January 20th*
_____ purpose or reason	*I am writing because . . .*
_____ salutation	*Dear Raquel,*
_____ your name	first name, or first and last name

D. **SEQUENCE** Read the parts of the letter and put them in the correct order. Write the correct number next to each part.

a. _____   I'll call you next week.

b. ___1___   March 12th

c. _____   This city is wonderful. The weather is warm most of the time. There are many parks, stores, and restaurants. There's good bus service. The bus goes around the city in an hour and stops near the shopping mall. The shopping mall has over a hundred stores, and I go there every day. The parks are very beautiful. There are a lot of palm trees and cactus plants.

d. _____   Dear Antonio,

e. _____   Raquel

f. _____   I am writing to tell you that I am staying with Marie in Palm City for one more week. I am having a lot of fun. Marie is very nice and kind. We went to the mall last night. Today, we walked in the park on her lunch break.

g. _____   Love,

E.   **Study the charts with your classmates and teacher.**

Simple Past (Regular)		
Subject	**Verb (base + *ed*)**	**Example sentence**
I, You, He, She, It, We, They	talked	I **talked** with Marie.
	wanted	She **wanted** a sandwich.
	walked	We **walked** in the park.

Simple Past (Irregular)		
Subject	**Irregular verb**	**Example sentence**
I, You, He, She, It, We, They	went (go)	I **went** to the park.
	ate (eat)	She **ate** at the coffee shop.
	bought (buy)	We **bought** new dresses.
	sent (send)	They **sent** a letter.

F.   **Fill in the blanks with the past tense form of the verbs in parentheses.**

1. I _____ (walk) to Marie's house.

2. You _____ (go) to school yesterday.

3. She _____ (send) me a letter from Palm City.

4. I _____ (want) a new sweater.

5. Raquel and Marie _____ (buy) new clothes at the store.

6. We _____ (eat) at the restaurant on Main and Carpenter.

G.   **APPLY   Complete the sentences.**

1. My city is _____.

2. There is a _____.

3. Every day, I _____.

4. Sometimes, I _____.

5. Yesterday, I _____.

6. Yesterday, I _____.

H.   **Write an e-mail and send it to a classmate.**

Where is the post office?

Before You Watch

A. Look at the picture and answer the questions.

1. Where is Naomi?

2. What is she doing?

While You Watch

B. ▶ **Watch the video. Circle the correct words to complete directions to the post office.**

1. First, take the number seven bus and (get down / ⟨get off⟩) at the mall.

2. Then, walk (towards / away from) the library.

3. Turn (left / right) on Nutwood.

4. Go (straight / around) three blocks.

5. The post office is (on / at) the left.

Check Your Understanding

C. Show the correct order of events by writing a number next to each sentence.

1. _____ A man sits on the bench.

2. _____ The man gives Naomi the directions and then gets on his bus.

3. __1__ Naomi is sitting by herself on the bench writing to Tara.

4. _____ Naomi writes to Tara that the people are very friendly.

5. _____ Naomi's bus arrives.

6. _____ Naomi asks for directions to the post office.

Review

A. Read the directions and follow the routes on the map. Write the names of the places where you arrive.

| post office | hospital | bank | library | pharmacy |

1. You are at the intersection of Montgomery and Vallejo. Go west on Vallejo for three blocks and turn left. Go one block. It's on the right. _____

2. You are at the intersection of Chestnut and Powell. Go south on Powell for one block. Then, go west on Lombard one block. It is across the street. _____

3. You are at the intersection of Broadway and Powell. Go south on Powell. Go two blocks and turn left. It's on the right. _____

4. You are at the intersection of Union and Mason. Go east on Union for two blocks. Then, turn left. It's on the right. _____

5. You are at the intersection of Green and Mason. Go west on Green for four blocks. Then, go north one block. It's on the corner. _____

B. Answer the questions.

1. Where can you send a package? _____

2. Where can you borrow a book? _____

3. Where can you buy gas for your car? _____

4. Where can you buy medicine? _____

5. Where can you eat a burger and french fries? _____

6. Where can you find a doctor? _____

7. Where can you report a crime? _____

8. Where can you register the birth of a new baby? _____

C. Read the paragraph. Fill in the blanks with the correct form of the verb *Be*.

This city _____ wonderful. The weather _____ warm

most of the time. There _____ many parks, stores, and restaurants. There

_____ good bus service. The bus goes around the city in an hour and stops

near the shopping mall. There _____ over a hundred stores in the shopping

mall, and I go there every day. The parks _____ very beautiful. There

_____ a lot of palm trees and beautiful flowers.

D. Read the e-mail. Circle the correct form of the verbs.

| Send | Save as Draft | Trash | Attachment | Signature |

From: sara@mai1.com

To: roberto@mai1.com

Cc:

Subject: Santa Barbara

Dear Roberto,

   I (write / am writing) to you from California. I (sit / am sitting) on the beach. I (stay / am staying) here in Santa Barbara with my friend, Suzanna. It's very warm and sunny. We (walk / are walking) on the beach every day. We often (eat / are eating) Mexican food in the evening. On weekends, we (visit / are visiting) beautiful places along the coast.

   Is it warm in Texas? I hope you (have / are having) a nice vacation there.

Your friend,

Sara

Learner Log

I can scan an Internet search page.   I can write and send a letter.
☐ Yes ☐ No ☐ Maybe   ☐ Yes ☐ No ☐ Maybe

E. Write down important locations. Look up their phone numbers online and add them to your list.

Location	Phone Number

F. Complete the profile and write a paragraph about what you did yesterday.

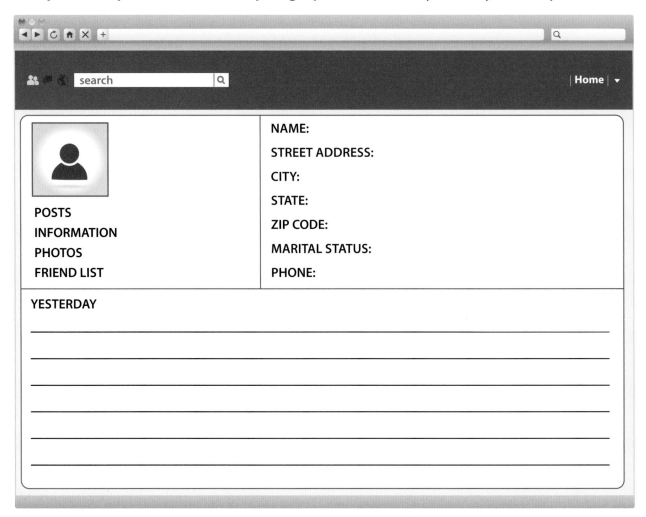

POSTS
INFORMATION
PHOTOS
FRIEND LIST

NAME:
STREET ADDRESS:
CITY:
STATE:
ZIP CODE:
MARITAL STATUS:
PHONE:

YESTERDAY
_____
_____
_____
_____
_____
_____
_____

✔ Describe your community

In a group, you are going to describe your community and write a postcard to a friend.

1. **COLLABORATE** Form a team with four or five students. In your team, you need:

Position	Job description	Student name
Student 1: **Team Leader**	Check that everyone speaks English. Check that everyone participates.	
Student 2: **Writer**	Write a paragraph about your community with help from the team.	
Student 3: **Artist**	Make a map of your community with help from the team.	
Students 4/5: **Spokespeople**	Prepare a class presentation with help from the team.	

2. Draw a map of the community around your school. Think about these questions:

- What buildings are there?
- What are the names of the streets?
- Is there a city bus? Where does it stop?

3. Write a paragraph about your community.

4. Write a postcard to a friend. Invite him or her to visit you.

5. Present your work to the class.

Planned towns have large residential areas.

EXPLORER DANIEL RAVEN-ELLISON

Guerrilla Geography

"Geography is about curiosity, exploration, and discovery. It gives you the power to see places in new ways, search for your own answers, challenge things as they are, and make sense of the world."
—Daniel Raven-Ellison

A. **INTERPRET** Complete the chart below with information from the pie chart.

Where Daniel spends time

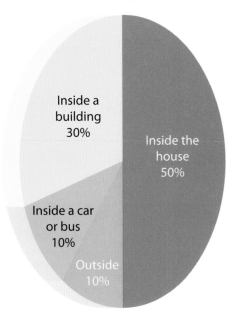

1. How much time does he spend inside the house?
   _____%

2. How much time does he spend inside a car or bus?
   _____%

3. How much time does he spend in a building?
   _____%

4. How much time does he spend outside?
   _____%

B. **CREATE** On a separate piece of paper, make a pie chart for yourself.

C. Read about Daniel Raven-Ellison.

Paragraph 1: Daniel Raven-Ellison is no ordinary geographer. He is a "guerrilla geographer." He is challenging everyone to explore the world around them in new and exciting ways. Some people think geography is learning about faraway places, but Daniel believes there is a lot to learn where people already live.

Paragraph 2: One of his projects is Mission: Explore. Mission: Explore is a geography education website that helps children have adventures in the town or city where they live. With Mission: Explore, children go on missions to learn about geography. Daniel wants children to get outside and see all there is to see. He wants them to experience all of life.

Paragraph 3: In 2014, Daniel started a project in the United Kingdom. He wanted to show people that they could climb enough steps to equal climbing Mount Everest without leaving the city, so he walked up the stairs of the tallest buildings in London until he climbed 29,029 feet or 8,848 meters! Many children are now finding stairs and counting steps today because of the project.

D. INFER Answer the questions about the main idea.

1. Which paragraph is about an adventure Daniel had? _____

2. Which paragraph is about Daniel's work? _____

3. Which paragraph is about the people Daniel cares about in his work? _____

E. CITE Answer the questions in a group. Underline the supporting ideas in the article.

1. Do you think Daniel likes children?

2. Did Daniel climb Mount Everest?

3. Does Daniel believe people need to visit faraway places to learn about geography?

F. APPLY Talk in a group about where you live. What do you like to do in your city?

Health

A 3D visualization of the Influenza A
virus, also known as "the flu"

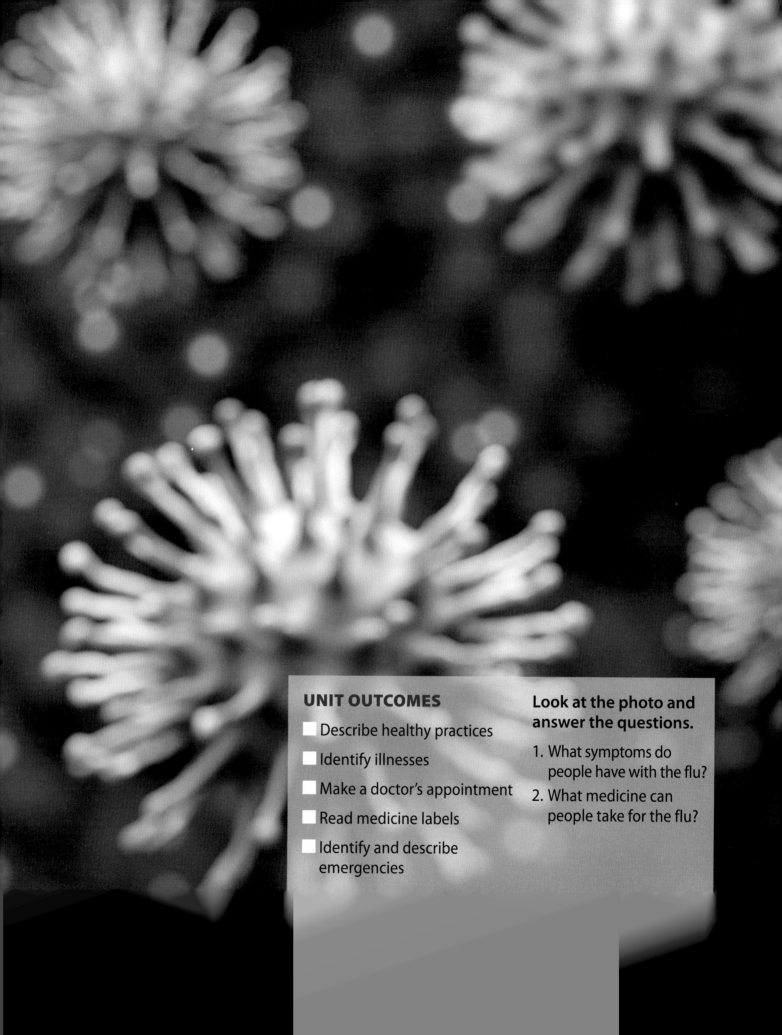

UNIT OUTCOMES

- Describe healthy practices
- Identify illnesses
- Make a doctor's appointment
- Read medicine labels
- Identify and describe emergencies

Look at the photo and answer the questions.

1. What symptoms do people have with the flu?
2. What medicine can people take for the flu?

LESSON ❶ A healthy life

A. **Match the questions to the pictures. Draw lines.**

How many hours of sleep do
adults and children need?

Is smoking healthy or unhealthy?
Why?

How much exercise do adults
need a day?

What is stress? What can people
do about stress?

B. **SURVEY** **Discuss the questions in Exercise A with your classmates and teacher.**
Complete the sentences below on a separate piece of paper.

Exercise: Our class thinks that adults need _____ hours of exercise a week.

Smoking: Our class thinks smoking is _____ because _____.

Stress: Our class thinks stress is when people worry a lot. We think people can _____.

Sleep: Our class thinks adults need _____ hours of sleep every night. We think that

children need _____ hours of sleep a night.

C. PREDICT What is the man's problem? What can he do?

D. Read the paragraph about stress.

> Many people have stress. Stress can make people tired, it can make them lose sleep, it can cause problems like high blood pressure, and it can even cause heart problems. There is a cure! Doctors say that good exercise, a proper diet, meditation, and rest can help with stress. Exercise and a good diet help people to think more clearly and to have more energy. When people exercise, they sleep better, too.

E. CLASSIFY Complete the table about stress.

Symptoms	Remedies (cures)
tired	

F. IDENTIFY Read the list below in a group. Check (✓) the healthy practices.

☐ eat three meals a day   ☐ play sports

☐ sleep twelve hours a night   ☐ eat a lot of candy

☐ work twelve hours a day   ☐ drink alcohol regularly

☐ smoke   ☐ rest and take breaks

☐ exercise every day

G. PREDICT Guess the missing information in the sentences. Then, listen to the lecture and check your answers.

CD 2
TR 12

1. Doctors say adults should exercise _____ minutes

   a _____.

2. Doctors say adults should eat _____ balanced meals a day.

3. Doctors say all adults should go in for a checkup _____ time(s)

   a _____.

4. Doctors say we should not _____.

5. Doctors say we should take _____.

H. Read the questions and circle the answers for yourself.

1. Are you tired during the day?   Yes   No

2. Do you need more sleep?   Yes   No

3. Do you have a good diet?   Yes   No

4. Do you take vitamins?   Yes   No

5. How many checkups do you have a year?   _____

Infinitives		
Subject	**Verb**	*to* + base verb
I	need	to exercise

I. APPLY Write your health goals.

EXAMPLE: I need to exercise 30 minutes every day.

_____

_____

_____

_____

_____

LESSON ② What's the matter?

GOAL ▮ Identify illnesses

A. IDENTIFY Look at the pictures and write the words.

shoulder(s)	mouth	neck	stomach	nose	lip(s)
head	tooth (teeth)	leg(s)	tongue	hand(s)	
foot (feet)	arm(s)	chest	eye(s)	ear(s)	

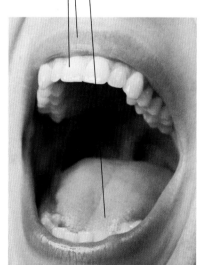

Simple Present

Possessive adjective	Body part		Example sentence
My	head (singular)		My head hurts.
Your	hand (singular)	hurts	Your hand hurts.
His	stomach (singular)		His stomach hurts.
Her	hands (plural)		Her hands hurt.
Our	shoulders (plural)	hurt	Our shoulders hurt.
Their	arms (plural)		Their arms hurt.

B. Practice the conversation. Make new conversations using the words in Exercise A.

Student A: What's the matter?
Student B: My <u>head</u> hurts.

C. Write the words from the box under the pictures. Then, listen and write the number of the conversation above each picture.

CD 2
TR 13–17

cough	sore throat	fever	headache	runny nose

_____   _____   _____   _____   _____

_____   _____   _____   _____   _____

D. Read the paragraph.

A cold and the flu are similar illnesses and have some of the same symptoms. The symptoms of a cold are a low fever, a sore throat, a headache, and a runny nose. People usually have a cold for one or two weeks. People with the flu feel very tired and sick. They often have a high fever, a dry cough, a headache, and muscle aches. Just like a cold, people can have the flu for one or two weeks, too. Many people get a cold or the flu every year and hate them both!

E. **CLASSIFY** Compare cold and flu symptoms. Complete the table.

Cold symptoms	Flu symptoms

F. Study the chart with your classmates and teacher.

Adjective	Comparative Adjective	Superlative Adjective
serious	more serious less serious	the most serious the least serious
common	more common less common	the most common the least common

G. **RANK** Look at the problems. Which ones are the most serious? Talk in a group and rank them from 1 to 8. Rank the most serious as *1*.

_____ a backache

_____ a cold

_____ a headache

_____ a runny nose

_____ a sore throat

_____ a stomachache

_____ a toothache

_____ the flu

H. **LIST** In a group, make a list of illnesses and symptoms that you think are the most common.

_____

_____

_____

_____

_____

_____

_____

_____

LESSON ③ Calling for an appointment

GOAL ▇ Make a doctor's appointment

A. PREDICT What is Alexi doing? Who is he talking to?

B. Read the story. What's the matter with Alexi? Why is he nervous?

My name is Alexi. I'm from Russia. I like school and I want to learn English, but I don't go to class very much. I'm tired a lot. I need to see a doctor, but I'm very nervous because I don't speak English well. My teacher says the doctor can help me.

C. PREDICT First, draw a line from the questions to the answers. Then, listen to the conversation to check your answers.

CD 2
TR 18

1. What's your name?	a. 1427 Hamilton Street, New York City
2. What's your date of birth?	b. Yes.
3. Why do you want to see the doctor?	c. Alexi Tashkov
4. What's your phone number?	d. No, I don't.
5. Where do you live?	e. (212) 555-5755
6. When can you see the doctor?	f. I'm tired all the time.
7. Do you have insurance?	g. Monday or Tuesday
8. Are you a new patient?	h. June 28, 1971

D. Study the charts with your classmates and teacher.

Simple Past (Regular)	
Subject	**Verb (base + *ed*)**
I, You, He, She, It, We, They	walked* (walk) talked* (talk) smoked* (smoke) played* (play)

Simple Past (Irregular)	
Subject	**Verb**
I, You, He, She, It, We, They	had (have) went (go) said (say)

*See the pronunciation note.

Simple Past: *Be*		
Subject	***Be***	**Example sentence**
I, He, She, It	was	I **was** sick.
You, We, They	were	You **were** at the hospital.

> **PAST TENSE**
>
> Notice how we pronounce the *ed* sound when speaking about the past.
>
> /t/ = walk/t/, talk/t/, smoke/t/
>
> /d/ = play/d/

E. Listen to Alexi. Then, listen again and write four sentences about his health habits using the past tense.

CD 2
TR 19

1. _____

2. _____

3. _____

4. _____

F. Listen to Alexi. Draw lines to make sentences.

CD 2
TR 20

1. He was	a. to smoke.
2. He went	b. to the doctor.
3. The doctor said	c. to stop smoking.
4. He continued	d. a heart attack.
5. He had	e. tired a lot.

G. CLASSIFY Listen and complete the table.

Name	Problem	Time and day	Method of payment
1. Alexi Tashkov			
2. Ming _____			
3. Michael _____			
4. Antonio Marco			
5. Sam _____			

H. APPLY Fill in the table with your information. Choose an illness from Lesson 2 or any other illness you can think of.

Name (What's your name?)	Problem (What's the matter?)	Time (When can you see the doctor?)	Method of payment (How will you pay?)

I. CREATE Use the information from Exercise H to make a conversation with your partner. Make an appointment to see the doctor.

Receptionist:	Hello, Alliance Medical Offices. Can I help you?
Sick Student:	Hello, I want to make an appointment to see Dr. Singh.
Receptionist:	OK. What's your name?
Sick Student:	_____
Receptionist:	_____
Sick Student:	_____
Receptionist:	_____
Sick Student:	_____
Receptionist:	_____
Sick Student:	_____

J. Perform your conversation for the class.

LESSON ④ Take two tablets

GOAL ▉ Read medicine labels

A. INTERPRET Find the words from the box on the medicine label and underline them.

directions	symptoms	uses	exceed	aches and pains
tablets	warning	reduce	persist	teenagers

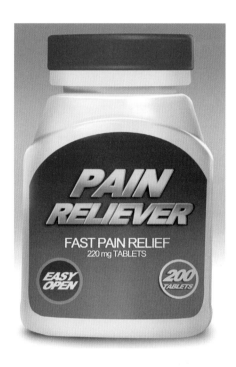

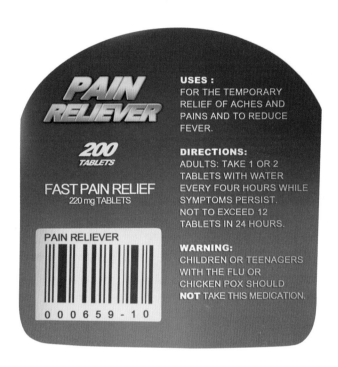

B. Match the words on the left with the examples on the right. Draw lines.

1. Directions   a. for relief of headaches

2. Uses   b. Don't drive.

3. Warning   c. Take two tablets.

C. DEFINE Match the words on the left with the definitions or examples on the right. Draw lines.

1. teenager   a. aches, pains, and fever

2. symptoms   b. continues

3. not to exceed   c. someone between the ages of 13 and 19

4. persists   d. no more than

D. **Look at the medicines with your classmates and teacher.**

a. cough syrup

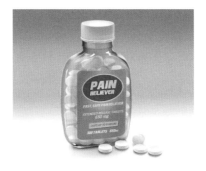

b. pain reliever

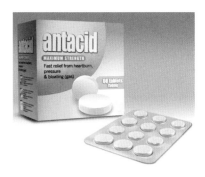

c. antacid

E. **IDENTIFY** **Write the letter of the correct medicine from Exercise D.**

_b_ **Uses:** for temporary relief of headaches or muscle aches and fever

_____ **Uses:** for temporary relief of coughs and throat irritation due to infections

_____ **Uses:** for fast relief of acid indigestion and stomach pain

_____ **Directions:** Chew 2–4 tablets as needed.

_____ **Directions:** Adults take one or two tablets with water every four hours while symptoms persist. Do not exceed 12 tablets in 24 hours.

_____ **Directions:** Take two teaspoons every four hours.

_____ **Warning:** Children or teenagers with the flu or chicken pox should NOT take this medicine.

_____ **Warning:** Do not chew more than 12 tablets in 24 hours.

_____ **Warning:** If throat pain persists or coughing is serious, contact your doctor.

SPOONS
tablespoon = 1/2 U.S. fluid ounce
teaspoon = 1/6 U.S. fluid ounce

Natural remedies, such as the hyssop plant, can be used to treat digestive problems.

F. **Study the chart with your classmates and teacher.**

Modal: *Should*			
Subject	*Should*	Base verb	Example sentence
I, You, He, She, It, We, They	should shouldn't	take drink chew swallow	I **should take** two tablets. He **shouldn't drink** alcohol with this medicine. She **should take** this medicine for a headache. You **shouldn't chew** this tablet. They **should swallow** this tablet with water.

🎧 **G.** **PREDICT Predict what statements are true about Alexi. Then, listen to the doctor's**
CD 2
TR 26 **instructions. Check (✓) what Alexi should do.**

  ☐ Alexi should take medicine and drive.

  ☐ He should take two pills three times a day.

  ☐ He should take the pills with water.

  ☐ He should take three pills two times a day.

  ☐ He should drink a little alcohol with the medicine.

  ☐ He should take aspirin and medicine as directed by a doctor.

H. **Read your answers to Exercise E. Write statements to describe what you should do with cough syrup. Use the statements for the pain reliever as a model.**

Pain reliever: You should take this medicine for temporary relief of headaches.

                 You should take one or two tablets every four hours.

                 Teenagers with chicken pox shouldn't take this medicine.

Cough syrup: _____

_____

_____

I. **APPLY Find a medicine label at home or on the Internet. Share its uses, directions, and warnings with the class.**

LESSON ⑤ It's an emergency!

GOAL ▮ Identify and describe emergencies

A. IDENTIFY Look at the emergencies. Label them *medical, police,* and *fire.*

1.

2.

3.

_____ _____ _____

B. INTERPRET Read the paragraph and pie chart about emergencies in Westmont Village.

Westmont Village is a beautiful town in New Mexico. It is very small, and there are not many emergencies. There is a very small hospital in Westmont Village. There are only 100 beds. The paramedics are also fire fighters. They take care of all the medical emergencies and fires. Last year, we had three small fires, 15 medical emergencies, and four robberies. We live in a very quiet town.

Emergencies in Westmont Village last year

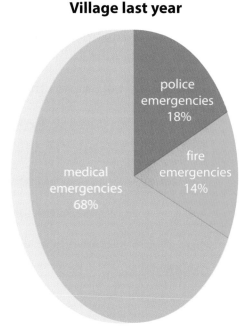

police emergencies 18%

fire emergencies 14%

medical emergencies 68%

C. Answer the questions about the paragraph and pie chart.

1. How many emergencies did Westmont Village have last year?

   a. 15   b. 3   c. 22

2. How large is the hospital?

   a. It's very large.   b. It's very small.   c. It's average size.

3. What percentage of emergencies are police emergencies?

   a. 14%   b. 68%   c. 18%

D. Listen and practice the conversation.

CD 2
TR 27

Operator:	911. What is your emergency?
Teresa:	It's a medical emergency.
Operator:	What's the problem?
Teresa:	My friend <u>is having chest pains.</u>
Operator:	I will send an ambulance immediately.
Teresa:	Thank you.
Operator:	What's your name and phone number? Where is your friend?
Teresa:	My name is <u>Teresa, and my cell number is 555-4334. The address is 9976 West Burma Street</u>. Please hurry!

Simple Past (Irregular)	
Base verb	**Past**
break	broke
drink	drank

E. Use the emergencies below to practice the conversation in Exercise D again.

1. is unconscious   2. is choking   3. drank poison

F.   **IDENTIFY**   **Listen to the conversations and circle the emergency in each one.**

CD 2
TR 28-31

1. robbery	car accident	fire
2. heart attack	fire	robbery
3. car accident	fire	robbery
4. fire	robbery	heart attack

G. **SURVEY** Read the table with your classmates and teacher. Underline the words you don't know. Complete the table in groups.

	Always call 911.	Never call 911.	Take medicine.	Brand name of medicine
She has a cold.		✓	✓	
A cat is in a tree.				
She has terrible chest pains.				
They have the flu.				
The man is not breathing.				
There is no food in the house.				
I am very tired.				
He coughs every day.				
She has a sore throat.				
She has a stomachache.				
She broke her arm.				
He accidentally drank poison.				

Advice	
You should	take call
You need	**to** take **to** call

H. Practice the conversation. Use the information in Exercise G to make new conversations.

Student A: What's the matter?
Student B: He accidently drank poison.
Student A: You need to call 911.

Before You Watch

A. Look at the picture and answer the questions.

1. Where are Hector and Mateo?

2. What's wrong with Mateo?

While You Watch

B. ▶ **Watch the video and complete the dialog.**

Hector:	I'm not sure. I—Oh, Mr. Patel, do we have any (1) _____ *aspirin* _____?

Mr. Patel: Let me guess. Mateo has a (2) _____?

Hector: How can you tell?

Mr. Patel: Let's check the first aid kit. Let's see. . . alcohol, iodine, (3) _____, tweezers . . . Here we are: ibuprofen, acetaminophen, aspirin.

Mateo: What's the difference?

Mr. Patel: They're very similar. They can all be used to treat headaches.

(4) _____ is a little stronger than the others, though.

Mateo: How much (5) _____ I take?

Check Your Understanding

C. Match each sentence with the appropriate response.

1. I have a cut.   a. Would you like some aspirin?

2. I have a headache.   b. Take some antacid.

3. My stomach hurts.   c. I'll get a pair of tweezers.

4. I'm very tired.   d. You'd better clean it with alcohol.

5. I have a splinter!   e. You should get some rest.

Review

A. Look at the picture and write the words.

B. Draw a line from the illness to the advice.

1. I have a headache.

2. I have a bad toothache.

3. I have a stomachache.

4. I have chest pains.

a. You should go to the dentist.

b. You should call 911 right now.

c. You should take a pain reliever.

d. You should chew some antacid tablets.

C. Give someone advice on how to stay healthy. Write two things the person should do and two things he or she shouldn't do. Use the pictures to help you.

should do

a. _____

b. _____

shouldn't do

a. _____

b. _____

D. Complete the sentences with the past tense form of the verbs in parentheses.

1. Yesterday, I _____ (have) a terrible headache.

2. Suzanne _____ (be) sick last week.

3. Last summer, we _____ (talk) to the doctor.

4. I _____ (go) to the hospital on Monday.

5. They _____ (call) the doctor five minutes ago.

6. Last year, the children _____ (be) sick a lot.

7. The doctor _____ (say) I shouldn't smoke.

8. He _____ (go) to the doctor's last week.

E. Match the section of the medicine label to the information. Draw lines.

1. Uses   a. Take two tablets three times a day.

2. Directions   b. Do not take more than 12 tablets in 24 hours.

3. Warning   c. for the temporary relief of aches and pains

F. Number the conversation in order.

_____ **Mario:** 66345 West Malvern Avenue.

_____ **Operator:** Is anyone injured?

_____ **Mario:** Yes, there is a fire.

___1___ **Operator:** 911. Can I help you?

_____ **Operator:** A fire? What's your name?

_____ **Mario:** I don't think so. Please hurry.

_____ **Mario:** Thank you!

_____ **Operator:** Yes, sir. They will be there very soon.

_____ **Operator:** Yes, of course. What is the address?

_____ **Mario:** Mario De la Vega. Please send the fire department.

G. Write the symptom under each picture and a possible medicine.

1.

Symptom: _____

Medicine: _____

2.

Symptom: _____

Medicine: _____

3.

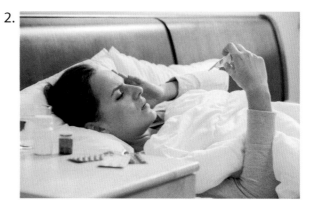

Symptom: _____

Medicine: _____

4.

Symptom: _____

Medicine: _____

In a group, you are going to design a health pamphlet for the community. The pamphlet will give health tips and explain what medicines to take for common illnesses.

1. **COLLABORATE** Form a team with four or five students. In your team, you need:

Position	Job description	Student name
Student 1: **Team Leader**	Check that everyone speaks English. Check that everyone participates.	
Student 2: **Nurse**	Give advice on medicines for three illnesses.	
Student 3: **Health Expert**	Give advice on three things to do to stay healthy.	
Students 4/5: **Artists**	Design pamphlet and prepare a class presentation with help from the team.	

2. Write three things people should do to be healthy. Write three things people should not do.

3. Think of three common illnesses to include in your pamphlet and describe them.

4. Write medicines people should take for these illnesses.

5. Design a pamphlet with pictures to present the information.

6. Prepare a presentation for the class.

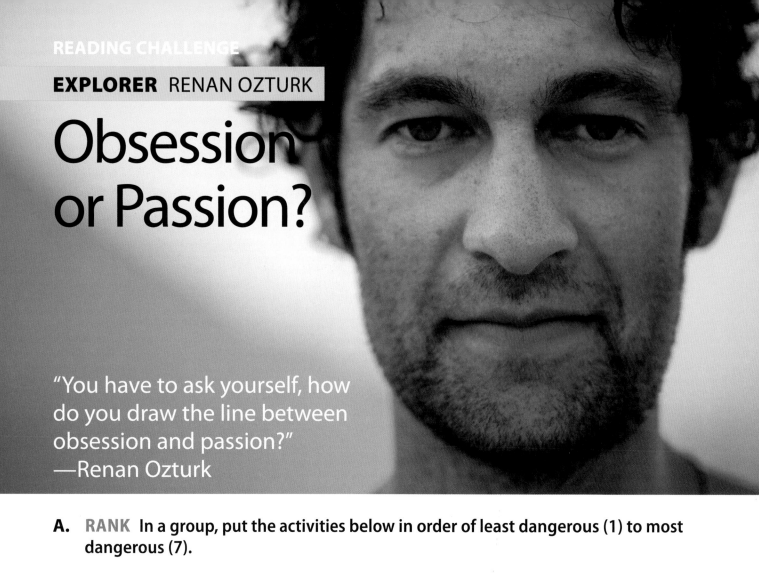

EXPLORER RENAN OZTURK

Obsession or Passion?

"You have to ask yourself, how do you draw the line between obsession and passion?"
—Renan Ozturk

A. **RANK** In a group, put the activities below in order of least dangerous (1) to most dangerous (7).

_____ exercising

_____ skiing

_____ rock climbing with ropes

_____ rock climbing with no ropes

_____ driving a car

_____ flying in a plane

__1__ watching TV

B. Check (✓) the things you would want to do if you were a filmmaker.

_____ film nature

_____ film people

_____ make movies

_____ make documentaries

C. Read about Renan Ozturk.

Paragraph 1: Renan Ozturk is a climber, filmmaker, and artist. He has climbed some of the world's most dangerous mountains. He often climbs with no ropes and only a little equipment. Renan likes to film his climbs and share his experiences with people. When he is climbing, Renan says to himself, "no mistakes," because just one mistake means he could die.

Paragraph 2: The dictionary defines *passion* as "having strong emotional beliefs." *Obsession*, on the other hand, means "unable to stop thinking about something." Renan is both passionate and obsessive about what he does. But how far can an obsession push someone?

Paragraph 3: In 2011, Renan had a terrible accident. He fell while skiing and filming in the Grand Tetons in Wyoming. He broke his neck and other bones, and he had a serious head injury. He almost died! Five months later, Renan began climbing again. He created a video of his recovery. The video starts with him in a neck brace and exercising. It ends with him taking off the neck brace and climbing again. Do you think what Renan does is an obsession or is it passion?

D. ANALYZE Each paragraph has a different idea. Write the number of the paragraph.

Accident and recovery _____   Renan's job _____   Obsession or passion? _____

E. Answer the questions.

1. What is the definition of *passion*?

_____

2. What is the definition of *obsession*?

_____

3. Why do you think Renan loves what he does?

_____

F. APPLY Take a class poll. Do you think Renan Ozturk is passionate or obsessed? Discuss as a class.

Work, Work, Work

A man paints the railing of a ship at sea.

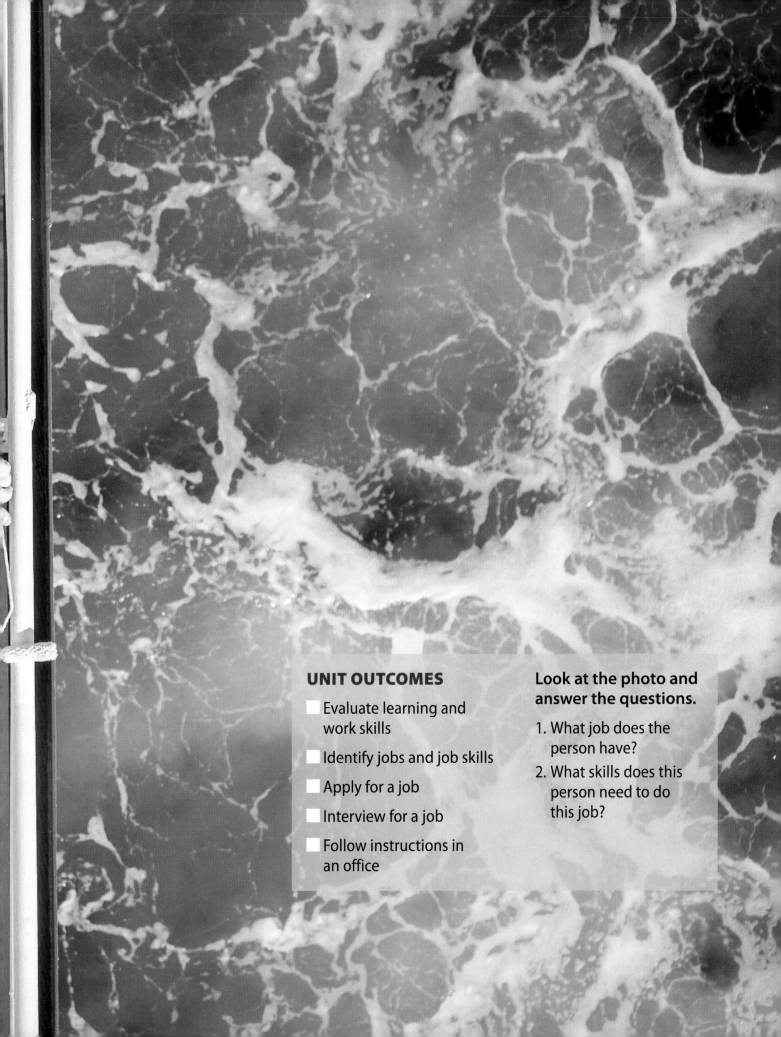

UNIT OUTCOMES

- [ ] Evaluate learning and work skills
- [ ] Identify jobs and job skills
- [ ] Apply for a job
- [ ] Interview for a job
- [ ] Follow instructions in an office

Look at the photo and answer the questions.

1. What job does the person have?
2. What skills does this person need to do this job?

LESSON **1** A good student and employee

GOAL ■ Evaluate learning and work skills

A. LIST What characteristics does a good student and a good employee have?

Student	Employee

B. Read about Dalva and good work habits. Underline any new words.

Dalva is an English student in Los Angeles, California. She needs a job. She had several jobs before she started studying. She was a cashier and an administrative assistant. She's a good worker and a good student. She comes to school on time every day, participates, and has a positive attitude. She helps other students and they help her.

Good work habits are very important in the United States. Employees who come on time, work hard, and cooperate are more successful than other employees. Good work habits in the classroom are similar to good work habits in the workplace.

C. EVALUATE Are you a good student with good work habits? Circle the number that best describes you.

	Always			Never
1. I come to class every day.	1	2	3	4
2. I come to class on time.	1	2	3	4
3. I participate in class and in groups.	1	2	3	4
4. I do my homework.	1	2	3	4
5. I listen carefully.	1	2	3	4
6. I help others.	1	2	3	4

D. INTERPRET Look at Dalva's employee evaluation form from 2008.

Fairview Hotel Employee Evaluation Form			
Name: Dalva Mendes			
Position: Administrative assistant			
Date: January 4th, 2008			
EVALUATION			
S = Superior	**G = Good**	**NI = Needs Improvement**	
1. Comes to work on time	S	G	NI
2. Follows instructions	S	G	NI
3. Helps others	S	G	NI
4. Works well with the team	S	G	NI
5. Understands the job	S	G	NI
Dalva is a new employee. She is still learning.			
6. Has a positive attitude	S	G	NI
Dalva enjoys her job and is always cheerful.			
Supervisor's signature: _____			
Employee's signature: _____			

E. Listen to the conversation between Dalva and her boss about her evaluation. Circle the correct information (*S*, *G*, or *NI*) on the form.

CD 2 TR 32

F. RANK In a group, talk about which characteristics are the most important to have at work. Number the characteristics from 1 to 6. *1* is the most important characteristic.

_____ Comes to work on time

_____ Follows instructions

_____ Helps others

_____ Works well with the team

_____ Understands the job

_____ Has a positive attitude

G. Study the charts with your classmates and teacher.

Future: *Will* (Affirmative)			
Subject	***Will***	**Base verb**	**Example sentence**
I, You, We, They, He, She, It	will	come listen help work have do	I **will come** to class on time. You **will listen** carefully and follow directions. He **will help** other students. She **will work** hard. We **will have** a positive attitude. They **will do** their homework.

Future: *Will* (Negative)			
Subject	***Will***	**Base verb**	**Example sentence**
I, You, We, They, He, She, It	will not (won't)	come leave forget	I **won't come** to class late. He **won't leave** class early. We **will not forget** our homework.

H. Complete the sentences with the future tense. Use the affirmative for things that are good to do at school. Use the negative for things that are bad to do at school.

1. I _____ will come _____ (come) to school on time every day.

2. Barry _____ (smoke) in class.

3. We _____ (participate) in groups.

4. You _____ (have) a positive attitude.

5. They _____ (forget) their notebooks.

6. I _____ (listen) carefully.

I.   PLAN Talk to a partner about two things you plan to do at school. Write your ideas and your partner's ideas using the future tense.

Me

1. _____

2. _____

My partner

1. _____

2. _____

LESSON ② What can you do?

GOAL ▊ Identify jobs and job skills

A. IDENTIFY Write each job title under the correct picture.

carpenter	construction worker	delivery person	mechanic
custodian	computer programmer	homemaker	administrative assistant

Kristina

1. _____

Esteban

2. _____

Ivan

3. _____

Salvador

4. _____

Clara

5. _____

Chang

6. _____

Natalia

7. _____

Phuong

8. _____

B. Practice the conversation. Make new conversations using the information in Exercise A.

Student A: What does Clara do?
Student B: She's an administrative assistant.

C. **Look at the tools. Discuss what they are used for with a partner.**

saw and hammer

wrench

broom and mop

copy machine

D. **CLASSIFY** **Look at the jobs below and write one or two tools for each job. Then, complete the skills using the words in the box.**

drives a truck	builds houses	delivers packages	writes programs
makes furniture	helps students	sends memos	cleans offices
fixes cars	listens carefully		

Job	Tool	Skill
carpenter		
computer programmer		
construction worker		
custodian		
delivery person		
driver		
mechanic		
office worker		
student		
teacher		

E. **INTERPRET** Dalva is interviewing for a job. Study the skills and job history sections of her job application. Then, listen and write the dates and job duties.

CD 2
TR 33

SECTION 2: SKILLS					
Computer Skills: word processing, presentation, and spreadsheet programs					
Languages: Spanish, French, Portuguese (fluent), and English (beginner)					
SECTION 3: JOB HISTORY					
Position	**Company**	**From**	**To**	**Duties**	
Administrative Assistant	Fairview Hotel				
Reason for Leaving I left to attend school.					
Position	**Company**	**From**	**To**	**Duties**	
Cashier	La Tostada Restaurant				
Reason for Leaving I moved.					

Can	*Can't*
I **can** type.	I **can't** type.
He **can** type.	He **can't** type.

F. According to Dalva's job application in Exercise E, what can she do? Write sentences about her skills.

1. She _____

2. _____

3. _____

4. _____

G. Talk to a partner. What can you do? What can your partner do?

You	**Your partner**
_____	_____
_____	_____
_____	_____

LESSON **3** Job hunting

GOAL ▪ Apply for a job

A. INTERPRET Scan for information. Write the correct jobs in the table below.

APARTMENT MANAGER

Full-time position for a bilingual (Spanish and English) apartment manager.
Must have two-years experience in painting and doing minor maintenance.

APPLY   MORE INFORMATION

FULL-TIME COOK

Full-time cook position at Martha's Kitchen.
No experience required as training will be given.
Good hours.

APPLY   MORE INFORMATION

CASHIER

Part-time cashier position at Franklin's Cinema.
$9.00 per hour.
No experience necessary.

APPLY   MORE INFORMATION

DRIVER

Full-time driver position for Alexander's Furniture Warehouse.
$10.00 per hour.
Clean driver's license required.
Monday–Friday, 6:00 a.m.–2:30 p.m.

APPLY   MORE INFORMATION

LEGAL ASSISTANT

Full-time position for a bilingual (Spanish and English) legal assistant at Smith and Peterson Law Offices.
Good organizational skills required.
Available immediately.

APPLY   MORE INFORMATION

ESL TEACHER

Part-time position for an ESL teacher at Casper Education Center.
BA and one-year teaching experience required.
Benefits available.

APPLY   MORE INFORMATION

BA
A **B**achelor of **A**rts degree is a degree from a university.

Information	Jobs
full-time	
part-time	
paid hourly	
needs a BA degree	
needs a driver's license	
needs no experience	

B. Ask and answer questions with a partner about the information in the ads in Exercise A.

EXAMPLE:

1. Is the apartment manager job full-time or part-time?

2. How much experience do you need for the apartment manager job?

3. How many languages do you need to speak for the apartment manager job?

C. COLLABORATE Read about the people below with your classmates and teacher. Practice pronunciation by emphasizing the words and syllables in bold. Then, with a partner, decide which job in Exercise A is best for each person.

> **STRESS**
>
> Place stress on words or syllables that are important in a sentence:
>
> *Who* is a hard worker?
>
> **SIL**via is a hard worker.
>
> *What kind of* worker is Silvia?
>
> Silvia is a **HARD** worker.

1. **Sil**via is a **hard** worker. She can work **full**-time or **part**-time. She speaks **Eng**lish well. She can work in an **office** and is **very** organized.

Job: _____

2. **Tanh** is **always** on time for **work**. He has a **driv**er's license and knows how to drive a **truck**.

Job: _____

3. **Let**i has **three** children and wants to stay **home** with them, but she needs to **work**. She can **fix** things around the house. Her **rent** is **very** expensive.

Job: _____

4. **Ri**go needs a **full**-time position. He **doesn't** have any experience. He wants to learn something **new**.

Job: _____

D. Listen to the people talking about the classified ads in Exercise A. Write the titles of the jobs they are talking about.

*CD 2
TR 34*

1. _____

2. _____

3. _____

4. _____

E. Match the questions and the correct responses. Draw lines.

Applicant	Employer
Excuse me. I am interested in the cashier position you are advertising.	Yes, here is one. Please fill it out and return it immediately.
Right. Do you have an application?	We are looking for someone to start immediately. Are you available?
Thank you. Are you hiring soon?	Perfect!
Yes. I can start right away.	The part-time position, right?

F. Practice the conversation in Exercise E with a partner.

G. APPLY Complete the application for yourself.

APPLICATION FOR EMPLOYMENT				
SECTION 1: PERSONAL INFORMATION				
Name:			Date:	
Address:				
Social security number:			Phone:	
Position applied for:				
SECTION 2: SKILLS				
Computer Skills:				
Languages:				
SECTION 3: JOB HISTORY				
Position	Company	From	To	Duties
Reason for Leaving				
Position	Company	From	To	Duties
Reason for Leaving				

LESSON ④ Job interviews

GOAL ■ Interview for a job

A. Dalva is interviewing for another job. Look again at her job history.

SECTION 3: JOB HISTORY				
Position	Company	From	To	Duties
Administrative Assistant	Fairview Hotel	December 2007	November 2008	
Reason for Leaving				
I left to attend school.				
Position	Company	From	To	Duties
Cashier	La Tostada Restaurant	June 2004	November 2007	
Reason for Leaving				
I moved.				

B. Listen to the conversation and circle *True* or *False*.

CD 2
TR 35

1. Dalva was a cashier at La Tostada Restaurant.   True   False

2. Dalva was a desk clerk at the Fairview Hotel.   True   False

3. Dalva answered the phone at the Fairview Hotel.   True   False

4. Dalva talked to guests at the Fairview Hotel.   True   False

C. Read and listen to the conversation. Check your answers to Exercise B.

CD 2
TR 36

Ms. Cardoza:	Good afternoon, Ms. Mendes. Please sit down. I have your application here. You were a desk clerk at the Fairview Hotel and before that you were a cashier. Is that right?
Dalva:	I was an administrative assistant at the Fairview Hotel. I wasn't a desk clerk.
Ms. Cardoza:	Oh, yes, that's right. What kind of work did you do?
Dalva:	I checked reservations and sent memos.
Ms. Cardoza:	So, you didn't answer the phone or talk to guests?
Dalva:	No, I didn't talk to guests, but I learn quickly and speak many languages.
Ms. Cardoza:	Did you work in the evenings?
Dalva:	No, I didn't work in the evenings. I finished at 6:30 p.m.
Ms. Cardoza:	Thank you, Ms. Mendes. We will call you.

D. Read about job interviews. Underline any new words.

The job interview is an important step in getting a job. Yes, the application is important—a well-presented application can help you get an interview, but a bad interview means no job! There are many things that interviewers are looking for in an interview. Among other things, the employer wants an employee who has a positive attitude and is confident. The employer knows that a worker with a good attitude will probably work hard and stay on the job.

The prospective employee will show confidence in many ways in the interview. For example, he or she will look the employer in the eye and give a firm handshake. He or she will speak confidently and listen carefully to the questions. The interviewee will also dress nicely and be prepared for the interview. All of these things—along with not smoking, eating, or chewing gum—will ensure a good interview.

E. SOLVE Match the new words with the definitions or examples. Draw lines.

1. along with	a. company; boss; supervisor
2. among other things	b. including
3. employee	c. possible in the future
4. employer	d. strong
5. firm	e. the person giving the interview
6. interviewee	f. the person in the interview who is looking for a job
7. interviewer	g. There are many things. One of them is this.
8. prospective	h. worker

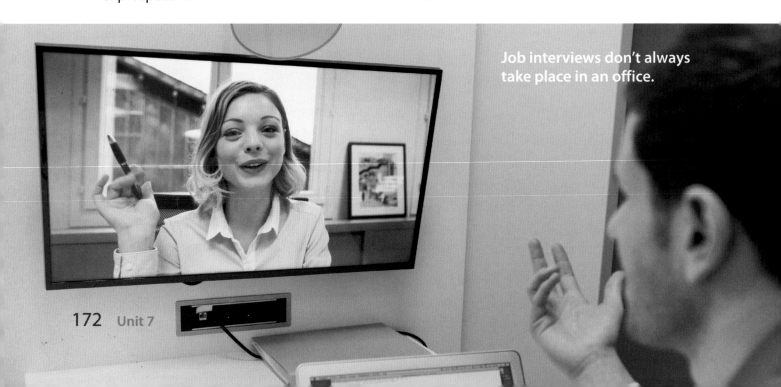

Job interviews don't always take place in an office.

F. Study the charts with your classmates and teacher.

Simple Past (Regular)	
Subject	**Past Verb (base + -ed)**
I, He, She, It We, You, They	checked worked cooked

Simple Past: *Be*	
Subject	**Be**
I, He, She, It,	was
We, You, They	were

Negative Simple Past (Regular)		
Subject	***Did + not***	**Base verb**
I, He, She, It, We, You, They	did not (didn't)	check work cook

Negative Simple Past: *Be*	
Subject	***Be + not***
I, He, She, It,	was not (wasn't)
We, You, They	were not (weren't)

G. Answer the questions using the negative simple past.

1. Was Dalva a student in 2008?

   Dalva _____ wasn't _____ a student in 2008. She was a student in 2009.

2. Did Dalva move in 2003?

   Dalva _____ in 2003. She moved in 2007.

3. Did Dalva work at the Fairmont Hotel?

   Dalva _____ at the Fairmont Hotel. She worked at the Fairview Hotel.

4. Did Dalva and Ms. Cardoza talk about the weather?

   Dalva and Ms. Cardoza _____ about the weather. They talked about Dalva's work experience.

5. Were Dalva and Ms. Cardoza at a restaurant?

   Dalva and Ms. Cardoza _____ at a restaurant. They were in an office.

6. Was Dalva late for the job interview?

   Dalva _____ late for the interview. She was on time.

H. CREATE With a partner, write a conversation that is a job interview. Share it with the class.

GOAL ▮ Follow instructions in an office

A. **IDENTIFY** Write the correct letter next to each machine in the picture.

a. fax machine	b. telephone	c. computer
d. shredder	e. printer	f. copier

🎧 **B.** **SEQUENCE** Listen to the instructions for the copier. Number the instructions in the
CD 2   correct order.
TR 37

_____ Choose the number of copies.

_____ Place the original on the glass.

___1___ Turn on the machine.

_____ Press the start button.

_____ Close the lid.

C. Write the names of the machines.

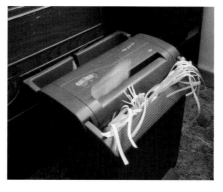

1. _____ 2. _____ 3. _____

D. Use the words from the box to complete the directions below. Then, write the names of the machines from Exercise C. You may use some of the words more than once.

connect	follow	keep	dial	turn on	turn off	print	press	place

Machine: _____

_____ the machine to a computer or a network.

_____ the instructions on your computer screen.

_____ your document.

Machine: _____

_____ the paper in the machine.

_____ the number.

_____ start.

Machine: _____

_____ the machine.

_____ the paper carefully in the slot.

_____ your fingers away from the machine.

_____ the machine after the paper is destroyed.

E. Study the chart with your classmates and teacher.

Imperatives		
	Base verb	**Example sentence**
~~you~~	place	**Place** the paper in the machine.
	enter	**Enter** the number.
	turn on	**Turn on** the computer.

F. We use imperatives to give instructions. Write out the instructions for the machines in Exercise C. Start each sentence with a verb.

Fax Machine Instructions

Place the paper in the machine. Dial the number. Press start.

Shredder Instructions

Printer Instructions

G. **APPLY** Talk in a group. Think of another machine (microwave, washing machine, vending machine, etc.) and write instructions.

LIFESKILLS ▶ Being on time is very important

Before You Watch

A. Look at the picture and answer the questions.

1. Where are Hector and Mr. Patel?

2. What is Mr. Patel telling Hector?

While You Watch

B. ▶ Watch the video and complete the dialog.

Mr. Patel: Well, better safe than sorry. Being on (1) _____*time*_____ for work is very important, especially when you are just starting.

Hector: Thank you, Mr. Patel. I'll work (2) _____ to get here early from now on.

Mr. Patel: That's good Hector. That's a very good (3) _____ to have. Having the right attitude is very important for a good employee. You seem to be doing a very good job so far.

Hector: Oh, I am. I really am (4) _____ my best to learn all about the job.

Mr. Patel: I can see that. Mateo and the other employees tell me you are very

(5) _____ and you listen carefully when learning new things.

Check Your Understanding

C. Match each sentence with the appropriate response.

1. I'm very pleased with your work.

2. You're late again.

3. What kinds of skills do you have?

4. We are behind schedule.

5. Your report has a lot of mistakes.

a. I'll stay late tonight and catch up.

b. I'll be more careful next time.

c. I can type and enter data.

d. Thank you. I try my best.

e. I'll be on time tomorrow.

Review

A. Look at the two sections from Youssouf's job application.

SECTION 2: SKILLS				
Computer Skills:				
Advanced programming; knowledge of many software programs				
Languages: French (bilingual)				

SECTION 3: JOB HISTORY				
Position	**Company**	**From**	**To**	**Duties**
Computer programmer	Datamix Computers	June 2014	Present	
Reason for Leaving				
Position	**Company**	**From**	**To**	**Duties**
Assembly worker	Datamix Computers	April 2010	May 2014	
Reason for Leaving				
Promotion				

B. Look at the skills section. Write sentences about what Youssouf can and can't do.

1. speak French   Youssouf can speak French. _____

2. speak Spanish   _____

3. build a house   _____

4. use software programs   _____

C. Look at Youssouf's job history. Complete the sentences with the correct negative or affirmative form of the verb in parentheses.

1. Youssouf _____ (work) at Datamix Computers in 2009.

2. Youssouf _____ (be) an assembly worker at Datamix Computers in 2012.

3. Youssouf _____ (start) his first job at Datamix in April 2010.

4. Youssouf _____ (be) a programmer from April 2010 to May 2014.

5. Youssouf _____ (change) his job in April 2014.

Learner Log

I can follow instructions in an office. I can evaluate learning and work skills.
■ Yes ■ No ■ Maybe   ■ Yes ■ No ■ Maybe

D. Identify the machines.

1. _____ 2. _____ 3. _____

E. Match the correct verb with the instruction.

_____ 1. Press   a. the paper in the machine.

_____ 2. Place   b. the number.

_____ 3. Dial   c. start.

F. Complete the sentences about school with the future (*will*) affirmative and negative.

1. I _____*will come*_____ (come) to work on time every day.

2. We _____ (eat) in class.

3. They _____ (play) basketball in class.

4. I _____ (work) with a partner.

5. You _____ (do) the homework every day.

6. They _____ (have) a good attitude.

7. She _____ (sleep) in class.

8. Dalva _____ (like) this class.

G. **Write the name of the job under the picture.**

1. _____

2. _____

3. _____

4. _____

5. _____

6. _____

H. **Read the classified ads. Complete the table below.**

HELP WANTED
Full-time custodian at John Adams School.
No experience needed.
$10 an hour.
Benefits included.

APPLY   MORE INFORMATION

HELP WANTED
Part-time mechanic.
One-year experience required.
$15.00 per hour.

APPLY   MORE INFORMATION

HELP WANTED
Full-time nurse position at Mayfield Hospital Tuesday through Saturday.
AA degree and one-year experience required.

APPLY   MORE INFORMATION

Position	Pay	Experience	Part-time/Full-time
1.			
2.			
3.			

In a group, you are going to make a new company. Write job advertisements and interview new employees.

1. **COLLABORATE** Form a team with four or five students. In your team, you need:

Position	Job description	Student name
Student 1: **Team Leader**	Check that everyone speaks English. Check that everyone participates.	
Student 2: **Recruiter**	Write a classified ad with help from the team.	
Student 3: **Designer**	Prepare an application form with help from the team.	
Students 4/5: **Interviewers**	Prepare interview questions with help from the team.	

2. You are the owners of a new company. What is the name of your company? What kind of company is it?

3. What job are you going to advertise? What information will you put in the advertisement?

4. What questions will you have on the application form? What questions will you ask at the job interview?

5. Interview four students for your job.

6. Decide who you will hire and present your work to the class.

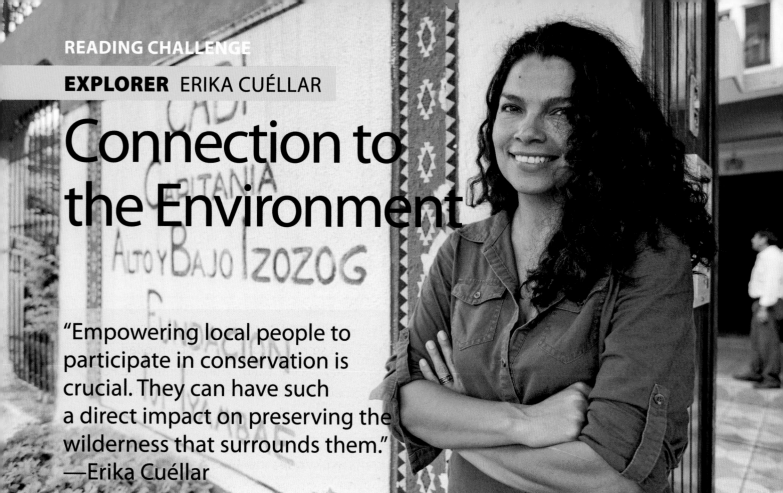

Connection to the Environment

"Empowering local people to participate in conservation is crucial. They can have such a direct impact on preserving the wilderness that surrounds them."
—Erika Cuéllar

A. PREDICT Draw a line from the word to the definition. Guess first and then use a dictionary to help you.

challenge	things around you
native	feeling good about yourself
environment	keep safe
pride	a problem or a difficult thing
protect	belonging to a place through birth

B. Use the words from Exercise A to complete the sentences.

1. I was born in Los Angeles, so I am a _____ of California.

2. It's natural for a mother to _____ her children from danger.

3. It is important to take care of the _____ for future generations.

4. As people get older, learning a language can be a _____.

C. Read about Erika Cuéllar.

Paragraph 1: We all know that education is important. Without it, people have trouble finding good jobs or starting a career. Education also teaches us about our role in the world. Protecting our environment is important and people's actions can sometimes damage the natural world. People who try to protect the environment and teach others about it are called *conservationists*. Erika Cuéllar is one conservationist who is trying to protect an important piece of land shared by four countries.

Paragraph 2: Erika is not only a conservationist. She is also a biologist. She is working to protect land in South America called the Gran Chaco. The Gran Chaco is part of Bolivia, Paraguay, Argentina, and a small part of Brazil. Uncontrolled development on this land is having a negative impact on the environment. For ten years, she worked with a team of scientists and with the native people who lived in part of the Gran Chaco in Bolivia. They all learned a lot, but Erika wants to do more.

Paragraph 3: Erika is training the native people to work and study the Gran Chaco so that they can teach others. The people have great pride in their education and many have good jobs. They are called *parabiologists*. They each studied more than 800 hours for certificates and have professional scientific conservation skills. Erika has made a big difference in their lives and she hopes they will make a big difference in the Gran Chaco.

D. Underline three of the words from Exercise A in the article. Then, write the sentences with the words on a separate piece of paper.

environment	native	pride

E. ANALYZE Answer the questions about details in the reading.

1. Where is the Gran Chaco?

a. In Bolivia, Uruguay, Argentina, and Brazil   b. In the United States

c. In South America   d. All of the above

2. What do you think the last sentence in the article means?

a. Erika doesn't live in the Gran Chaco.   b. Erika is different.

c. Erika helped people and the environment.   d. Erika is a biologist.

F. APPLY Talk to a group of students. What education do you need for your dream job?

Goals and Lifelong Learning

At 90 years old, Iris Apfel became a visiting professor at the University of Texas at Austin.

UNIT OUTCOMES

- Identify goals
- Set academic goals
- Set work goals
- Find ways to learn
- Record goals

Look at the photo and answer the questions.

1. What do you think this woman does? Why?
2. What goals do you think this woman has?

LESSON ❶ **What is success?**

GOAL ■ Identify goals

A. Read and discuss the questions.

> What is success? Some people think success is a good job and a lot of money. Others say it is love and family. What is success to you?

B. RANK What is most important to you? Number the items from 1 to 6. *1* is the most important to you.

_____ family   _____ employment

_____ money   _____ friends

_____ entertainment   _____ education

C. Read about what is important to Marie.

My career is important to me. I plan to study nursing and work part time as a home health-care aide. Then, I am going to get my degree in nursing and become a registered nurse. My family life is also important to me. I will save some money because I want to get married soon. My boyfriend's name is Jean. After we get married, we plan to have children. I will work hard to reach my goals

D. RANK In a group, rank what you think is important to Marie. Number the items from 1 to 6. *1* is the most important. Then, share your ideas with another group.

_____ family   _____ employment

_____ money   _____ friends

_____ entertainment   _____ education

E. PREDICT Where is Carmen? What is she doing?

F. PREDICT Check (✓) Carmen's goals. Then, listen and check your answers.

CD 2
TR 38

☐ buy a house	☐ get a job	☑ study English
☐ move	☐ keep a job	☐ participate in child's school
☐ get married	☐ learn new skills at work	☐ get a high school diploma
☐ have children	☐ get a promotion	☐ go to college
☐ become a citizen	☐ get a better job	☐ graduate from college

G. CLASSIFY Look at Carmen's goals in Exercise F. Write them in the correct boxes.

Personal and family

Vocational (work)

Academic (educational)

She wants to study English.

H. Study the charts with your classmates and teacher.

Future Plans: *Want to, Hope to, Plan to*		
Subject	**Verb**	**Infinitive** (*to* + base)
I, You, We, They	hope, want, plan	to study in school for three years
He, She	hopes, wants, plans	to graduate from college to get married

Future Plans: *Be going to*		
Subject	***Be going to***	**Base verb**
I	am going to	get a high school diploma
You, We, They	are going to	participate in class
He, She	is going to	buy a house

	want to	*hope to*	*plan to*	*be going to*	
less definite	←			→	more definite

I. Complete the sentences expressing future plans with the correct forms of the verbs.

1. Carmen and Marie _____ want to speak _____ (want / speak) English.

2. I _____ (plan / come) to class on time every day.

3. Marie _____ (hope / be) a nurse someday.

4. Lien _____ (be going to / graduate) from college.

5. Marco and I _____ (plan / visit) Mexico in the future.

6. They _____ (want / move), but they have a three-year lease.

J. **PLAN** Write two future plans for you and a partner.

My future plans

_____

_____

My partner's future plans

_____

_____

LESSON ② Education in the United States

GOAL ■ Set academic goals

A. INTERPRET Discuss the pie chart with your classmates and teacher.

Education levels in the United States

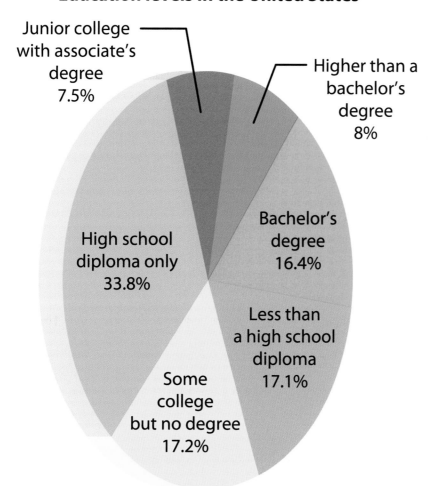

Junior college with associate's degree 7.5%

Higher than a bachelor's degree 8%

High school diploma only 33.8%

Bachelor's degree 16.4%

Some college but no degree 17.2%

Less than a high school diploma 17.1%

B. Practice the conversation. Make new conversations using the information in the pie chart.

Student A: What percentage of people in the United States have less than a high school diploma?
Student B: 17.1%

C. PLAN Write one academic goal that you have. Use the ideas on page 187 and one of the ways to express future plans on page 188.

_____

_____

D. Listen to the lecture. Then, read and discuss the educational choices adults have in the United States.

CD 2
TR 39

High School Diploma
Some adult schools have high school classes where you can earn a high school diploma.

Certificates
Certificates for specific trades like nursing, computer programming, and mechanics can be earned from trade schools, some junior colleges, and some adult schools.

BA/BS Degree
This is called a Bachelor of Arts or a Bachelor of Science degree. Adults earn this degree from a four-year college or university.

GED
Some adult schools have classes to help you prepare for a test. If you pass the test, you earn a GED, or General Equivalency Diploma. This diploma is similar to a high school diploma.

AA/AS Degree
This is called an Associate of Arts or an Associate of Science degree. Adults earn this degree from a two-year junior or community college.

Graduate Degree
After earning a bachelor's degree, adults can study more and receive additional degrees.

Adult Schools
These schools are sometimes free. Students learn basic skills like reading and writing. They can learn about jobs and computers. These schools can help students get their GED.

Junior Colleges/Community Colleges
These schools are not expensive for residents. They offer two-year academic, technical, and vocational courses. They help students prepare for universities or jobs. Students can study part time in the evenings or on the weekends.

Colleges/Universities
These schools prepare students for jobs and careers. They are often very expensive. They offer four-year academic courses.

Trade Schools
These schools are sometimes expensive. They help students learn job-related skills, such as computers or mechanics.

E. Work with a partner. Circle *True* or *False* for each statement.

1. It is necessary to have a BA or a BS before you can get a graduate degree.	True	False
2. You can receive a high school diploma from some adult schools.	True	False
3. AA degrees are from four-year schools.	True	False
4. You can earn a GED in high school.	True	False
5. You can earn a certificate in trade schools.	True	False
6. You can earn a bachelor's degree from any adult school or college.	True	False

F. Read the following paragraphs again in Exercise D: *Adult Schools, Junior Colleges/Community Colleges, Colleges/Universities,* and *Trade Schools.* Match the questions with the answers.

1. __*b*__ Why is it good to get a high school diploma?

2. _____ Why do people go to a two-year college?

3. _____ Why do people go to a university?

4. _____ Why do people go to an adult school?

a. to learn how to read and write English or to get a GED

b. to get a better job or prepare to go to a two-year college or university

c. to get an Associate's degree, to get a better job, or to prepare to go to a university

d. to qualify for a career or to get a Bachelor's degree

G. Study the chart with your classmates and teacher.

Because			
Statement	**Reason**		
	Because	**Subject + verb**	**Information**
Marie plans to go to college		she wants	to be a nurse.
Lien hopes to learn English	because	she plans	to go to college.
They hope to go to an adult school		they want	to learn English.
I want to go to a trade school		I want	to be a mechanic.

H. **PLAN** Write an academic goal. Use *because* and write why you want to reach this goal.

_____

_____

_____

_____

_____

_____

_____

_____

LESSON **3** Workplace goals

GOAL ▮ Set work goals

🎧 **A. Listen to and read about Lien's work goals.**

CD 2
TR 40

> Lien has many goals. She wants to have a career. She wants to be a counselor in an adult school or a college because she wants to help people. She needs to go to school for many years to study, but first she needs to learn English. She will go to Clear Mountain Adult School for two more years. She is going to learn English and get a GED. Lien also needs to work. She needs a part-time job now, and later she plans to work at a school for more experience.

B. INTERPRET Study the timeline and talk about Lien's plans with a partner.

Lien's Plan					
2016	**2018**	**2019**	**2020**	**2022**	**2024**
Go to Clear Mountain Adult School Get a part-time job	Take the GED Start Mountain Heights Community College	Get a part-time job as a teacher's aide	Transfer to a university	Get a part-time job in the career office of the university	Graduate from university with a BA degree Get a job as a counselor

EXAMPLE: **Student A:**   What does Lien plan to do in 2016?
Student B: She plans to go to Clear Mountain Adult School and get a part-time job.

It's never too late to continue your education.

C. Study the charts with your classmates and teacher.

Future: *Will*			
Subject	***Will***	**Base verb**	**Information**
I, You, He, She, It, We, They	will	go	to school for two more years.
		study	English this year.

	want to	*hope to*	*plan to*	*be going to*	*will*	
less definite	←				→	more definite

D. COMPARE Look at the diagram and write sentences about Lien's and Marie's future plans.

Lien
- take the GED
- become a teacher's aide
- become a counselor

Lien and Marie
- work part time
- study English at Clear Mountain Adult School
- go to college
- get a college degree

Marie
- become a registered nurse
- work in a hospital

1. Lien is going to become a counselor.
2.
3.
4.
5.
6.
7.
8.
9.

E. PREDICT What does Mario do? What do you think his plan is?

F. INTERPRET Read Mario's timeline.

Mario's Plan			
2016	**2017**	**2018**	**2019**
Go to Clear Mountain Adult School	Get a part-time job in an automobile shop	Go to a community college and study auto mechanics and accounting	Start an auto-repair business

G. PREDICT Match the statements with the reasons. Write the letters next to the statements. Then, listen and check your answers.

_____ 1. Mario wants to get a part-time job in an automobile shop

a. because he wants to be self-employed.

_____ 2. Mario needs to start his auto-repair business

b. because he wants to study auto mechanics and accounting.

_____ 3. Mario needs to go to Clear Mountain Adult School

c. because he wants to learn English.

_____ 4. Mario plans to go to a community college

d. because he wants experience in auto repair.

H. PLAN Write a work goal. Use *because* and write why you want to reach this goal.

_____

_____

LESSON ④ Lifelong learning

GOAL ▪ Find ways to learn

A. PREDICT Ahmed is wearing a yellow shirt. Why isn't he sitting with the other students? How does he feel?

B. Read Ahmed's story.

Ahmed's first day at Clear Mountain Adult School was difficult. He didn't speak English, and many students only spoke Spanish or Portuguese. He wanted to go home, but he didn't. He went to school every day. He worked hard and listened carefully. Now, he can speak and understand English.

C. SOLVE Look at Ahmed's problems and find the solutions. Draw a line from the problem to the solution. There is more than one solution for every problem.

Problems

1. didn't speak English

2. wanted a high school diploma

3. wanted to go to the library

4. didn't have a job

Solutions

a. asked a friend for help

b. looked in the newspaper

c. went to school every day

d. worked hard and listened carefully

e. called for the address

f. looked on a map

g. talked to a counselor

D. **Study the chart with your classmates and teacher.**

Past with *So*			
Base	**Negative** *didn't* + **base verb**	**Affirmative**	**Example sentence**
ask	didn't ask	asked*	He didn't speak English, **so** he asked for help.
go	didn't go	went	She didn't speak English, **so** she went to school.
Pronunciation: *ask/t/			

E. **PREDICT** **Predict what Ahmed did to resolve his problems. Then, listen and check your answers.**

CD 2
TR 42

Problem	Ask a friend	Talk to the police	Go to school	Look in the phone book	Go to the library	Talk to a counselor	Ask the teacher	Look online in a newspaper
1. He didn't speak English.	X		X		X			
2. He didn't have a job.								
3. He didn't know what to do in an emergency.								
4. He didn't know where to find information about citizenship.								
5. He needed to find a home for his family.								
6. He needed to find a school for his children.								

F. **On a separate piece of paper, write sentences about Ahmed. Use *so*.**

EXAMPLE: _Ahmed didn't speak English, so he went to school._

G. How can the resources below help you to learn? Draw lines. There can be more than one answer.

1. the public library   a. get advice on health and legal problems

2. the Internet   b. borrow books or videos

3. hotline   c. take classes in English, computer programming, or art

4. an adult education center   d. read the latest news and find jobs

H. **INTERPRET** Read the flyer.

Come to the Mountain View Public Library

OPEN: Monday–Thursday 9–9, Friday and Saturday 9–5, Sunday 1–5

The Mountain View Public Library has books, DVDs, and CDs for adults and children of every age. Our staff will help you search our computer catalogs or access the Internet. Our collection includes books in more than 40 languages.

Join one of our book discussion groups or try our creative writing workshop. Come to one of our lunchtime lectures to learn how to start your own business or to learn about countries around the world with one of our guest speakers.

For more information about our services, come to the information desk at the main entrance. Our services are free to all state residents.

I. List the things you can do at the Mountain View Public Library.

1. *You can borrow books, DVDs, and CDs.* _____

2. _____

3. _____

4. _____

J. **APPLY** Tell a group where you go for help when you have a problem. Look at Exercise E for examples of problems.

LESSON 5 My goals

GOAL ▮ Record goals

A. **INFER** Look at the pictures. What are Marie's plans in each picture?

1. _____

_____

2. _____

_____

3. _____

_____

4. _____

_____

B. Listen and write the sentences in order.

CD 2
TR 43

First, _Marie plans to study nursing and work part time as a home health-care aide._____.

Second, _____.

Third, _____.

Fourth, _____.

C. Read the goals below. Check (✓) any goals you have.

- ☐ buy a house
- ☐ move
- ☐ get married
- ☐ have children
- ☐ become a citizen

- ☐ get a job
- ☐ keep a job
- ☐ learn new skills at work
- ☐ get a promotion
- ☐ get a better job

- ☐ study English
- ☐ participate in child's school
- ☐ get a high school diploma
- ☐ go to college
- ☐ graduate from college

D. **COMPARE** Talk to a partner and complete the diagram.

My goals   **Our goals**   **My partner's goals**

_____   _____

_____   _____

_____   _____

_____   _____

_____   _____

_____

Some people plan to become citizens of the United States.

E. Study the paragraph and the correct formatting with your classmates and teacher.

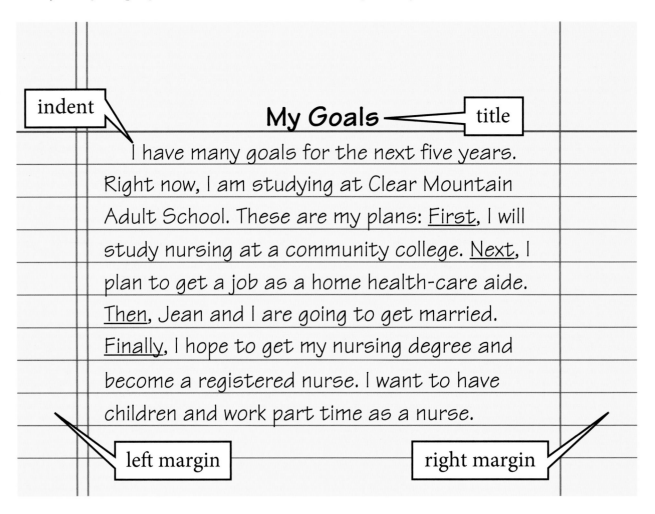

indent

My Goals — title

I have many goals for the next five years. Right now, I am studying at Clear Mountain Adult School. These are my plans: <u>First</u>, I will study nursing at a community college. <u>Next</u>, I plan to get a job as a home health-care aide. <u>Then</u>, Jean and I are going to get married. <u>Finally</u>, I hope to get my nursing degree and become a registered nurse. I want to have children and work part time as a nurse.

left margin

right margin

F. Read the paragraph again. Look at the underlined words. What do they show?

G. PLAN Write your plans for the next five years.

First, I _____ .

Next, _____ .

Then, _____ .

Finally, _____ .

H. CREATE Write a paragraph about your goals. Use the example paragraph In Exercise E as a model. When you are finished, share it with the class.

LIFESKILLS ▶ Sounds like a good plan

Before You Watch

A. Look at the picture and answer the questions.

1. Where are Naomi, Hector, and Mateo?

2. What does Naomi have in her hands? Why?

While You Watch

B. ▶ **Watch the video and complete the dialog.**

Naomi: Well, it's called a "self-help book." It teaches you how to (1) _____ goals and achieve them.

Hector: That sounds interesting. What does it say?

Naomi: It says here, "It is becoming more and more difficult to get a good job and make enough money. To be (2) _____ in life, you need to set goals."

Mateo: That (3) _____ sense. Goals give your life a sense of direction.

Mr. Patel: That's right! "First, you need to (4) _____ your goal. Then, you need to make a plan for achieving your goal."

Hector: Could you explain that a little more?

Naomi: You can't just cross your fingers and say, "I hope my dreams come true." You have to make a plan that goes (5) _____ -by-step.

Check Your Understanding

C. Write the steps Naomi, Mateo, and Hector plan to take to achieve their goals.

Naomi	Mateo	Hector
1. *go to art school*		
2. *get an internship*		
3. *become a graphic artist*		

A. Complete the paragraph about the educational system in the United States. Use the words from the box.

associate's	bachelor's	community	diploma	elementary

Children in the United States start _____ school at five or six years old.
Next, they usually go to a junior high school or middle school, and then to high school. When they
finish high school, they receive a _____. After that, they can get a job, or
go to a junior college or a _____ college for two years, where they get a(n)
_____ degree. They can also go to a university for four years and get a(n)
_____ degree.

B. Match the words with the definitions. Write the correct letter next to each word.

_____ 1. resident   a. finish high school or college

_____ 2. vocational   b. person who advises other people

_____ 3. counselor   c. related to studying

_____ 4. academic   d. person who lives in a country or state

_____ 5. graduate   e. related to your job

C. Ask three friends about their goals. Write sentences about them.

1. _____

_____

2. _____

_____

3. _____

_____

D. **Read about Teresa. Use the words from the box to label the parts of the paragraph.**

| indent | left margin | title | right margin |

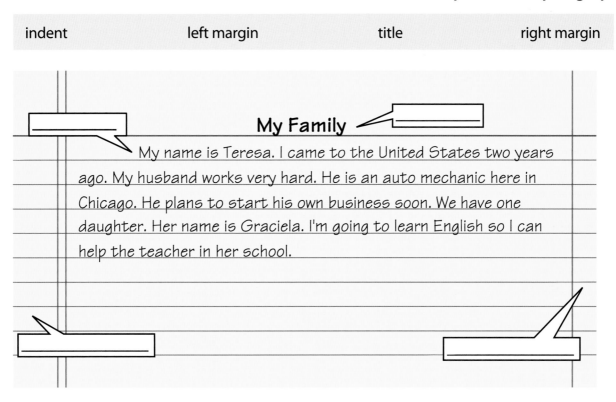

My Family

My name is Teresa. I came to the United States two years ago. My husband works very hard. He is an auto mechanic here in Chicago. He plans to start his own business soon. We have one daughter. Her name is Graciela. I'm going to learn English so I can help the teacher in her school.

E. **Write a paragraph about yourself. Use *plan to, hope to, want to, going to,* and *will* to talk about your future plans. Choose one of the titles below.**

1. My Family   2. My Job   3. My Goals

Learner Log

I can identify goals.	I can set work goals.	I can find ways to learn.
▇ Yes ▇ No ▇ Maybe	▇ Yes ▇ No ▇ Maybe	▇ Yes ▇ No ▇ Maybe

F. Read the goals and write *P/F* for personal or family goals, *V* for vocational goals, and *A* for academic goals.

1. __A__ get a high school diploma

2. _____ travel around the world

3. _____ learn programming at a trade school

4. _____ have two children

5. _____ get a part-time job

6. _____ buy a house

7. _____ read a novel

8. _____ work in a doctor's office

G. List resources where you can find information.

_____   _____

_____   _____

H. Use the correct forms of the words in parentheses to express future plans.

1. Kimberly _____ (will) work in a doctor's office someday.

2. Paul and Kimberly _____ (be going to) have a baby.

3. She _____ (hope to) finish school before the baby comes.

4. He _____ (want to) get a better job before the baby comes.

5. They _____ (plan to) build a new baby's room onto their home.

I. Complete the sentences about yourself.

1. I want to _____.

2. I hope to _____.

3. I plan to _____.

4. I am going to _____.

5. I will _____.

TEAM PROJECT ✓ Make a timeline

In a group, you are going to make a timeline of your goals.

1. **COLLABORATE** Form a team with three or four students.

2. Draw a timeline for your group for the next five years.

3. Each team member writes three goals on pieces of paper and puts them on the timeline.

4. Show your timeline to the other groups.

Portfolio

You are going to write a paragraph and make a timeline of your goals to include in your personal portfolio.

1. Make a timeline on a large piece of paper. On your timeline, write what you want to do for the next five years.

2. Write a paragraph about your family.

3. Write a paragraph about what you are doing now in your life.

4. Write a paragraph about your plans for the next five years.

5. Show your paragraphs to a friend and ask for comments. Use the comments to improve your writing.

6. Make a cover sheet for your timeline and your paragraphs.

7. Present your portfolio to the class and read your paragraphs.

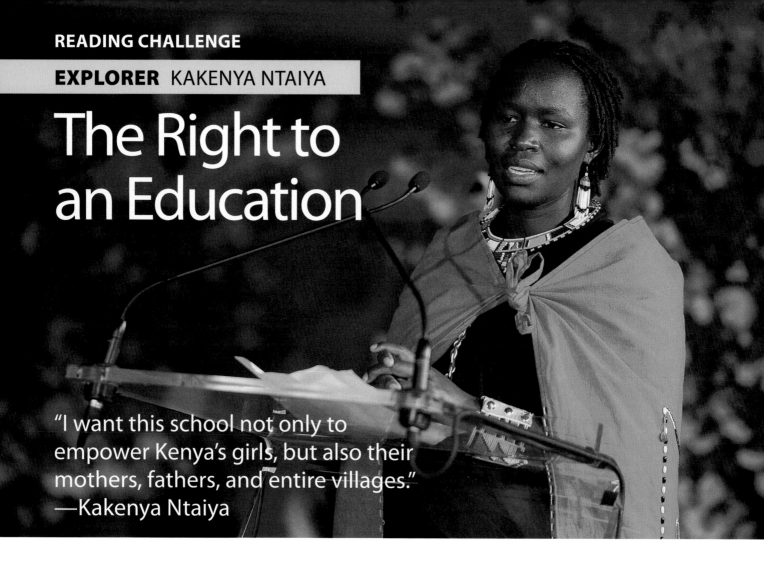

EXPLORER KAKENYA NTAIYA

The Right to an Education

"I want this school not only to empower Kenya's girls, but also their mothers, fathers, and entire villages."
—Kakenya Ntaiya

A. **APPLY** Look at the adjectives below. Mark the ones that describe you. Use a dictionary for words you don't know.

confident	strong	bold
courageous	fearless	enthusiastic
happy	persistent	hard-working

B. Write sentences about yourself.

EXAMPLE: _I am confident._

_____

_____

_____

_____

C. Read about Kakenya Ntaiya.

Kakenya Ntaiya is an educator and activist who grew up in a Maasai village in Kenya. In her village—like many Maasai villages—young girls marry when they are 12 or 13 years old, and they don't go to high school. This kind of life didn't appeal to Kakenya because she wanted to continue her education. She had to convince her father to allow her to go to high school, but when she wanted to go to college in the United States, she had to convince everyone in her village. Kakenya wanted to make a difference, and she promised the village that she would come back and help, so they collected money for her to go.

After college, Kakenya came home confident and fearless. She decided to convince the village yet again. This time, she wanted to build a school for girls. Kakenya understands that education is important and can help everyone, and now in Kakenya's small village, one building is making a difference: an elementary school for girls. "I want this school not only to empower Kenya's girls, but also their mothers, fathers, and entire villages." Kakenya set an example for others to follow and she teaches people who want to make a difference.

D. ANALYZE What are four problems or challenges Kakenya had to face?

1. _____

2. _____

3. _____

4. _____

E. On a separate piece of paper, make a list of challenges you face that make it difficult to go to school.

F. APPLY Write a paragraph about what you want to do in the future. Use the future tense and the adjectives from Exercise A.

_____

_____

_____

_____

_____

Faces of India

Men celebrate the Holi festival in Rajasthan, India.

Over the last eight units, you have met lots of new people. You have learned where they come from, where they live, and what they do. You are now going to learn about some more new people thanks to photographer Steve McCurry.

Before You Watch

A. **Which words are parts of the face? Circle the correct answers.**

lips	back	shoulder	mouth	eyes	legs
arm	nose	foot	fingers	knee	stomach

B. **Look at the map of India. Then, complete each sentence with the correct answer.**

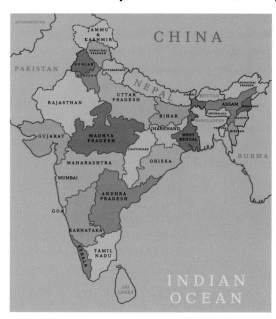

1. Sri Lanka is _____ of India.
   a. northeast   b. northwest
   c. southwest   d. southeast

2. Nepal is _____ of India.
   a. northeast   b. northwest
   c. southwest   d. southeast

3. Mumbai is in the _____ of India.
   a. north   b. south
   c. east   d. west

4. Rajasthan is in the _____ of India.
   a. northeast   b. northwest
   c. southwest   d. southeast

C. **Look at the jobs and definitions. Complete each sentence with the correct word.**

fortune teller	person who tells stories about the future
snake charmer	person who can control snakes, usually with a musical instrument
magician	person who performs magic tricks
shepherd	person who feeds and cares for large groups of animals, usually sheep
photographer	person who takes pictures with a camera

1. Michael asked the _____ to tell him about his future.

2. The _____ pulled two white rabbits out of a small black hat.

3. Twenty young sheep followed the _____ from his farm to the village.

4. The snake danced while the _____ played music.

5. A _____ took pictures of my sister and her husband at their wedding.

While You Watch

A. Read the jobs and look at the pictures from the video. Write the correct job under each picture.

shepherd	snake charmer	photographer	fortune teller

a. _____

b. _____

c. _____

d. _____

B. Watch the video again. Look for the tools people use to do their jobs. Match the tool to the job.

___ 1. photographer   a. rocks

___ 2. snake charmer   b. camera

___ 3. shepherd   c. stick

___ 4. fortune teller   d. musical instrument

C. Steve McCurry thinks that Rajasthan, India is a beautiful place. Make a short list of the beautiful things you see in the video. Then, share your list with the class.

_____

_____

_____

_____

_____

After You Watch

> **WORD FOCUS**
>
> In the video, Steve McCurry says that he is a *shy* person. The word *shy* can mean *nervous* or *afraid*. *Nervous* and *afraid* are **synonyms**. Synonyms are words that have almost the same meaning.

A. Read the information in the box above and read the words below. Circle three synonyms for the word *job*.

career	eyes	job	newspaper	profession	school	village
college	face	music	position	religion	travel	work

B. Write a one-paragraph letter about Steve McCurry's job. Then, share your letter with a classmate. Use the synonyms for the word *job* where you can.

Dear _____,

_____

_____

_____

_____

_____

_____

C. Did you learn anything new from the video? Fill in the table with new information that you learned. Then, discuss as a class.

New Information	
India	**Photographers**

STAND OUT VOCABULARY LIST

PRE-UNIT
Feelings
angry 4
happy 4
hungry 4
nervous 4
numbers 7
sad 4
tired 4

UNIT 1
Family
aunt 18
brother 18
daughter 18
father 18
granddaughter 18
grandfather 18
grandmother 18
husband 18
mother 18
nephew 18
niece 18
parents 18
sister 18
son 18
uncle 18
wife 18
Personal information
eyes 20
hair 20
heavy 20
height 20
old 22
short 20
tall 20
thin 20
weight 20
young 22
Weather
cloudy 26
foggy 26
rainy 26
snowy 26
sunny 26
windy 26

UNIT 2
Clothing
baseball cap 41
blouse 39

boots 41
coat 39
dress 39
gloves 41
jacket 39
pants 39
sandals 41
scarf 41
shirt 39
shorts 41
skirt 39
sneakers 47
socks 39
sunglasses 41
sweater 39
tie 39
t-shirt 41

UNIT 3
Menus
beverage 63
dessert 63
main course 63
salad 63
sandwich 63
side order 63
soup 63
Containers and units
bag 66
baking needs 68
bottle 66
box 66
can 66
canned goods 68
checkout 68
carton 66
dairy 68
frozen foods 68
gallon 66
jar 66
loaf 66
meats 68
pound 66
produce 68
supermarket 68
Food groups
dairy 71
fruit 71
grains 71
protein 71
vegetables 71

Meals
breakfast 72
dinner 72
lunch 72
Cooking verbs
add 75
boil 75
chop 75
cook 75
drain 75
mix 75
peel 75
whip 75

UNIT 4
Housing and rooms
apartment 87
balcony 89
bathroom 95
bedroom 95
condominium 87
dining room 95
house 87
kitchen 95
living room 95
mobile home 87
pool 89
yard 95
Furniture
armchair 96
bookcase 96
coffee table 96
couch 96
dining room table 96
dresser 96
end table 96
lamp 96
washer/dryer 96
Banking
ATM 98
cash 98
deposit 98
withdraw 98

UNIT 5
Public services
bank 116
bowling alley 114
city hall 116
clothes store 116
courthouse 116

department store 116
fast-food restaurant 116
fire station 116
gas station 116
hardware store 116
hospital 116
library 116
movie theater 114
pharmacy 116
police station 116
post office 116
shoe store 116
supermarket 116

UNIT 6
Parts of the body
arm 141
back 141
chest 141
ear 141
eye 141
foot 141
hand 141
head 141
heart 141
leg 141
lip 141
mouth 141
neck 141
nose 141
shoulder 141
stomach 141
tongue 141
tooth (teeth) 141
Symptoms
backache 143
cough 142
fever 142
headache 142
runny nose 142
sore throat 142
stomachache 143
toothache 143
Medicine labels
aches and pains 147
directions 147
exceed 147
persist 147
reduce 147
symptoms 147
tablets 147

teenagers 147
uses 147
warning 147
Medicines
antacid 148
cough syrup 148
emergencies 150
pain reliever 148

UNIT 7
Jobs
administrative
   assistant 167
carpenter 165

cashier 167
computer programmer
   165
construction worker 165
cook 168
custodian 165
delivery person 165
driver 168
homemaker 165
manager 167
mechanic 165
office worker 165
Tools
broom 166

hammer 166
mop 166
saw 166
wrench 166
Office machines
computer 174
copier 174
fax machine 174
printer 174
shredder 174

UNIT 8
Education
adult school 190

Associate's Degree 190
Bachelor's Degree 190
certificate 190
college 190
community college 190
diploma 190
GED (General Equivalency
   Diploma) 190
graduate 190
trade school 190
university 190

IRREGULAR VERB LIST

Base Verb	Simple Past	Base Verb	Simple Past
be	was, were	give	gave
bring	brought	go	went
build	built	have	had
buy	bought	make	made
choose	chose	meet	met
come	came	put	put
do	did	read	read
drive	drove	see	saw
drink	drank	send	sent
draw	drew	sleep	slept
eat	ate	speak	spoke
feel	felt	teach	taught
find	found	write	wrote

STAND OUT GRAMMAR REFERENCE

Be Verb to Express Feelings

Subject	*Be*	Feelings	Example sentence
I	am	fine	I **am** fine. (I'**m** fine.)
You, We, They	are	nervous sad tired happy	You **are** nervous. (You'**re** nervous.) We **are** sad. (We'**re** sad.) They **are** tired. (They'**re** tired.)
He, She, It	is	angry hungry	He **is** angry. (He'**s** angry.) She **is** hungry. (She'**s** hungry.)

Possessive Adjectives

Pronoun	Possessive adjective	Example sentence
I	My	**My** address is 3356 Archer Blvd.
You	Your	**Your** phone number is 555-5678.
He	His	**His** last name is Jones.
She	Her	**Her** first name is Lien.
We	Our	**Our** teacher is Mr. Kelley.
They	Their	**Their** home is in Sausalito.

Questions with *Can*

Can	Pronoun	Verb	Example sentence
Can	you	help answer repeat say speak spell	Can you help me? Can you answer the question? Can you repeat that, please? Can you say it again, please? Can you speak slower? Can you spell it, please?

Simple Present: *Be*

Subject	Verb	Information	Example sentence
I	am	from Mexico	I **am** from Mexico.
We, You, They	are	single 23 years old	We **are** single. You **are** 23 years old.
He, She	is	divorced	He **is** divorced. She **is** from Vietnam.

Simple Present: *Have*

Subject	Verb	Information
I, You, We, They	have	three brothers two sisters
He, She	has	no cousins three sons

Comparative and Superlative Adjectives

Adjective	Comparative adjective	Superlative adjective
tall	taller	the tallest
short	shorter	the shortest
heavy	heavier	the heaviest
thin	thinner	the thinnest
old	older	the oldest
young	younger	the youngest

Simple Present

Subject	Verb	Information	Example sentence
I, You, We, They	eat go help play	lunch to school with the children soccer	I **eat** lunch at 4:00 p.m. You **go** to school at 8:00 a.m. We sometimes **help** with the children. They **play** soccer on Saturday.
He, She	eat**s*** goe**s**** help**s*** play**s****	lunch to school with the children soccer	He **eats** lunch at 12:00 p.m. Nadia **goes** to school at 10:00 a.m. Gilberto **helps** with the children. She **plays** soccer on Friday.

Pronunciation: */s/   **/z/

Negative Simple Present

Subject	Negative	Base verb	
I, You, We, They	don't		
		wear	sandals
He, She	doesn't		

Imperatives

	Base verb	Example sentence
~~you~~	drain	**Drain** the water.
	chop	**Chop** the potatoes.
	peel	**Peel** the potatoes.

Negative Imperatives

	Negative	Base verb	Example sentence
~~you~~	do not don't	boil	**Do not boil** the water. (**Don't boil** the water.)
		use	**Do not use** salt. (**Don't use** salt.)
		cook	**Do not cook** in the microwave. (**Don't cook** in the microwave.)

Imperatives

	Base verb		Example sentence
~~you~~	**go**	straight straight ahead	**Go** straight three blocks. **Go** straight ahead.
	turn	left right around	**Turn** left on Nutwood. **Turn** right on Nutwood. **Turn** around.
	stop	on the left on the right	**Stop** on the left. **Stop** on the right.

Information Question	Answer
How much is the house?	It's $1,200 a month.
What kind of housing is Number 2?	It's a mobile home.
Where is the condominium?	It's on Shady Glen.
How many bedrooms does the apartment have?	It has three bedrooms.

Information Questions

What is your name?	**How** long did you live there?
Where do you live now?	**Who** is your employer?
Where did you live before?	**What** is your position?

Modals: *May* and *Might*

Subject	Modal	Base verb	Example sentence
I, You, He, She, We, They	may might	spend earn	I **may** spend $50 on gasoline this month. They **might** spend $300 a month on food. We **may** earn $3,500 a month.

Present Continuous

Subject	*Be*	Base verb + *ing*	Example sentence
I	am	writing	I **am writing** this letter in English.
You, We, They	are	going	We **are going** to the mall.
He, She	is	eating	He **is eating** at the coffee shop.

Simple Past (Regular)

Subject	Verb (base + *ed*)	Example sentence
I, You, He, She, It, We, They	talked wanted walked	I **talked** with Marie. She **wanted** a sandwich. We **walked** in the park.

Simple Past (Irregular)

Subject	Irregular verb	Example sentence
I, You, He, She, It, We, They	went (go) ate (eat) bought (buy) sent (send)	I **went** to the park. She **ate** at the coffee shop. We **bought** new dresses. They **sent** a letter.

Infinitives

Subject	Verb	to + base verb
I	need	to exercise

Modal: *Should*

Subject	*Should*	Base verb	Example sentence
I, You, He, She, It, We, They	should shouldn't	take drink chew swallow	I **should take** two tablets. He **shouldn't drink** alcohol with this medicine. You **should take** this medicine for a headache. She **shouldn't chew** this tablet. They **should swallow** this tablet with water.

Future Plans: *Want to, Hope to, Plan to*

Subject	Verb	Infinitive (*to* + **base**)
I, You, We, They	hope, want, plan	to study in school for three years
He, She	hopes, wants, plans	to graduate from college to get married

Future Plans: *Be going to*

Subject	*Be going to*	Base verb
I	am going to	get a high school diploma
You, We, They	are going to	participate in class
He, She	is going to	buy a house

Future: *Will* (Affirmative)

Subject	*Will*	Base verb	Example sentence
I, You, He, She, It, We, They	will	come listen help work have do	I **will come** to class on time. You **will listen** carefully and follow directions. He **will help** other students. She **will work** hard. We **will have** a positive attitude. They **will do** their homework.

Future: *Will* (Negative)

Subject	*Will*	Base verb	Example sentence
I, You, He, She, It, We, They	will not (won't)	come leave forget	I **won't come** to class late. He **won't leave** class early. We **will not forget** our homework.

Because

Statement	Reason		
	Because	Subject + verb	Information
Marie plans to go to college	*because*	she wants	to be a nurse
Lien hopes to learn English better		she plans	to go to college

Past with *So*

Base	Affirmative	Negative *didn't* + base verb		Example sentence
ask	asked *	didn't	ask	He didn't speak English, **so** he asked for help.
go	went	didn't	go	She didn't speak English, **so** she went to school.
Pronunciation: *ask/t/				

Simple Past (Regular)

Subject	Past Verb (base + -*ed*)
I, He, She, It We, You, They	checked worked cooked

Simple Past: *Be*

Subject	*Be*
I, He, She, It,	was
We, You, They	were

Negative Simple Past (Regular)

Subject	*Did* + *not*	Base verb
I, He, She, It, We, You, They	did not (didn't)	check work cook

Negative Simple Past: *Be*

Subject	*Be* + *not*
I, He, She, It,	was not (wasn't)
We, You, They	were not (weren't)

PHOTO CREDITS

Cover Image: Mark Edward Atkinson/ Tracey Lee/Getty Images, Bottom Images (Left to Right) Jay B Sauceda/Getty Images, Tripod/Getty Images, Portra Images/Getty Images, Portra Images/Getty Images, Dear Blue/Getty Images, Hero Images/ Getty Images, Jade/Getty Images, Seth Joel/Getty Images, LWA/Larry Williams/ Getty Images, Dimitri Otis/Getty Images, **2** (tl) (tc) Portra Images/Getty Images, (tr) Mark Edward Atkinson/Tracey Lee/Getty Images, (cl) Hero Images/Getty Images, (c) Jade/Getty Images, (cr) Seth Joel/ Getty Images, **7** (t) Michael Newman/ PhotoEdit, (c) (b) David Young-Wolff/ PhotoEdit, **9** (tl) STOCK4B/Getty Images, (tr) Dennis Kitchen Studios, Inc./PhotoEdit, (cl) Jose Luis Pelaez Inc/Getty Images, (cr) George Doyle/Stockbyte/Getty Images, **12–13** Guillaume Chanson/Getty Images, **14** (l) Tony Freeman/PhotoEdit, (c) Blend Images - John Lund/Sam Diephuis/Getty Images, (r) David Young-Wolff/PhotoEdit, (background) Chrupka/Shutterstock.com, **15** (l) David Young-Wolff/PhotoEdit, (c1) Blend Images - John Lund/Sam Diephuis/ Getty Images, (c2) Tony Freeman/PhotoEdit, (r) Michael Newman/PhotoEdit, **17** (tl) (tr) Paul Thomas/Riser/Getty Images, (c1) Hans Neleman/Stone/Getty Images, (c2) Bill Bachmann/PhotoEdit, (c3) Hanover David Young-Wolff/PhotoEdit, (c4) bikeriderlondon/Shutterstock.com, (c5) David /The Image Bank/Getty Images, (c6) Peter Hendrie/The Image Bank/ Getty Images, (bl) (br2) Michael Newman/ PhotoEdit, (br1) Mary Kate Denny/ PhotoEdit, **18** (t1) (t3) (t4) (c3) Paul Thomas/ Riser/Getty Images, (t2) (c2) (b2) Michael Newman/PhotoEdit, (c1) Bill Bachmann/ PhotoEdit, (c4) (b4) Mary Kate Denny/ PhotoEdit, (b1) Peter Hendrie/The Image Bank/Getty Images, (b3) Hans Neleman/ Stone/Getty Images, **23** Rocketclips, Inc./ Shutterstock.com, **26** Bisams/Shutterstock .com, **28** (tl) Songquan Deng/Shutterstock .com, (tr) Dusan Milenkovic/Shutterstock .com (c1) Tom Mareschal/Alamy Stock Photo, (c2) fstockfoto/Shutterstock.com, (bl) ArTDi101/Shutterstock.com, (br) kohy/ Shutterstock.com, **29** © Cengage Learning, **30** (l) David Litschel/Alamy Stock Photo, (r) Blend Images - John Lund/Sam Diephuis/ Getty Images, **31** (tl) David Litschel/ Alamy Stock Photo, (tr) Blend Images - John Lund/Sam Diephuis/Getty Images, (c1) (b2) Tony Freeman/PhotoEdit, (c2) (b1) Myrleen Pearson/PhotoEdit, (c3) (c4) Michael Newman/PhotoEdit, (b3) Myrleen Ferguson Cate/PhotoEdit, **34** © Neil Losin, **36–37** Kris Davidson/National Geographic Creative, **43** Nata Sha/Shutterstock.com,

49 Liam Norris/Getty Images, **53** © Cengage Learning, **57** Ira Berger/Alamy Stock Photo, **58** Bill Hatcher/National Geographic Creative, **60–61** Edwin Remsberg/VWPics/ Redux, **62** Minerva Studio/Shutterstock. com, **63** (tl1) JaroPienza/Shutterstock.com, (tl2) Jacek Chabraszewski/Shutterstock. com, (tl3) oknoart/Shutterstock.com, **66** (t1) janecocoa/Getty Images, (t2) Gts/ Shutterstock.com, (t3) 5PH/Shutterstock. com, (t4) artem_ka/Shutterstock.com, (c1) M. Unal Ozmen/Shutterstock.com, (c2) Aleksie/Shutterstock.com, (c3) Kunertus/ Shutterstock.com, (c4) Stacey Newman/ Shutterstock.com, (bl) Enlightened Media/ Shutterstock.com, **67** Elena Shashkina/ Shutterstock.com, **72** (bl) JGI/Blend Images/ Jupiter Images, (br) Caterina Bernardi/The Image Bank/Getty Images, (cl) Bananastock/ JupiterImages, (br) Baoba Images/Riser/ Getty Images, (bl) Minerva Studio/iStock/ Getty Images Plus/Getty Images, **74** Nitr/ Shutterstock.com, **75** HandmadePictures/ Shutterstock.com, **77** © Cengage Learning, **78** (tl) Stockcreations/Shutterstock.com, (tr) Brent Hofacker/Shutterstock.com, (cl) cobraphotography/Shutterstock.com, (cr) Lesya Dolyuk/Shutterstock.com, **79** (cl1) 5PH/Shutterstock.com, (cr1) Enlightened Media/Shutterstock.com, (cl2) janecocoa/ Getty Images, (cl2) artem_ka/Shutterstock .com, (bl1) Aleksie/Shutterstock.com, (br1) Kunertus/Shutterstock.com, (bl2) Stacey Newman/Shutterstock.com, (br2) Gts/ Shutterstock.com, **80** Slawomir Fajer/ Shutterstock.com, **81** cultura/Corbis, **82** Marvin Joseph/The Washington Post/ Getty Images, **84–85** © Inter IKEA Systems BV 2014, **87** (cl) pbk-pg/Shutterstock. com, (cr) Konstantin L/Shutterstock.com, (bl) Iriana Shiyan/Shutterstock.com, (br) Atlaspix/Shutterstock.com, **88** (l) Baoba Images/Riser/Getty Images, (r) Tony Freeman/PhotoEdit, **96** (t1) Ad Oculos/ Shutterstock.com, (t2) StudioSmart/ Shutterstock.com (t3) lynnette/Shutterstock .com, (t4) Room27/Shutterstock.com, (c1) Sandratsky Dmitriy/Shutterstock.com, (c2) donatas1205/Shutterstock.com, (c3) Zhukova Valentyna/Shutterstock.com, (c4) James Marvin Phelps/Shutterstock.com, **97** Artazum and Iriana Shiyan/Shutterstock .com, **101** © Cengage Learning, **103** Paul Maguire/Shutterstock.com, **106** Gordon Wiltsie/National Geographic Creative, **108** © Tristram Stuart, **109** (c1) (c) (cr) (bl) (bc) (br) Missions Media/National Geographic Creative, **111** (tl) Tyrone Turner/National Geographic Creative, (tc1) Stephen Dorey ABIPP/Alamy Stock Photo, (tc2) J. Baylor Roberts/National Geographic Creative, (tr) Gordon Wiltsie /National

Geographic Creative, **112–113** © Lynda Cosgrave, **114** Jon Bilous/Shutterstock .com, **116** (cl) Meinzahn/Getty Images, (c) Ken Wolter/Shutterstock.com, (cr) Hxdbzxy/ Shutterstock.com, **129** © Cengage Learning, **133** Kent Weakley/Shutterstock.com, **134** Darren Moore/National Geographic Creative, **136–137** Science Picture Co/ Science Source, **138** (tr) racorn/Shutterstock .com, (cr1) PathDoc/Shutterstock.com, (cr2) Blend Images/Shutterstock.com, (br) SirinS/Shutterstock.com, **139** Jasminko Ibrakovic/Shutterstock.com, **141** (t) Air Images/Shutterstock.com, (b) Vibe Images/ Shutterstock.com, **142** (t1) Bananastock/ JupiterImages, (t2) MIXA/Getty Images, (t3) Goodluz/Shutterstock.com, (t4) Stockbyte/ Getty Images, (t5) Custom Medical Stock Photo/Alamy Stock Photo, **148** Alis Photo/ Shutterstock.com, **150** (tl) Photographee .eu/Shutterstock.com, (tc) Konovalov/ Shutterstock.com, (tr) Brian A Jackson/ Shutterstock.com, **151** (cl) Andrey_Popov/ Shutterstock.com, (c) Juanmonino/E+/Getty Images, (cr) Photographee.eu/Shutterstock .com, **153** © Cengage Learning, **154** Greg Epperson/Shutterstock.com, **155** (tl) Blend Images/Shutterstock.com, (tc1) SirinS/ Shutterstock.com, (tc2) racorn/Shutterstock .com, (tr) PathDoc/Shutterstock.com, **156** (cl) Antonio Guillem/Shutterstock.com, (cr) Photographee.eu/Shutterstock.com, (bl) Lisa F. Young/Shutterstock.com, (br) Kaspars Grinvalds/Shutterstock.com, **158** Jimmy Chin/National Geographic Creative, **160–161** © Zay Yar Lin, **162** Andresr/ Shutterstock.com, **166** (tl) Vasko Miokovic Photography/E+/Getty Images, (tc1) akkara sookthip/Shutterstock.com, (tc2) Oote Boe Ph/Alamy Stock Photo, (tr) Sylvie Bouchard/Shutterstock.com, **172** LDprod/ Shutterstock.com, **175** (tl) FabrikaSimf/ Shutterstock.com, (tc) John T. Fowler/Alamy Stock Photo, (tr) leungchopan/Shutterstock .com, **177** © Cengage Learning, **179** (tl) FabrikaSimf/Shutterstock .com, (tc) John T. Fowler/Alamy Stock Photo, (tr) leungchopan/Shutterstock. com, **182** © Rolex Awards/Thierry Grobet, **184–185** Chester Higgins Jr./The New York Times/Redux, **186** Cheryl Savan/ Shutterstock.com, **187** Zero Creatives/ cultura/Corbis, **192** Digital Vision./Getty Images, **194** Grove Pashley/Getty Images, **199** Mike Segar/Corbis, **201** © Cengage Learning, **206** Michael Loccisano/Getty Images Entertainment/Getty Images, **208** Steve McCurry/Magnum Photos, **209** Tupungato/Shutterstock.com, **210** (tl) (tr) (cl) (cr) National Geographic Learning.

STAND OUT SKILLS INDEX

ACADEMIC SKILLS

  Charts, graphs, and maps, 8, 16, 19, 21, 22, 27–28, 49, 51, 64, 67, 73, 87, 114, 115, 119, 122, 130, 139, 143, 145, 152, 164, 189, 191, 193, 196

    Plurals, 66–67

  Critical Thinking

    Analyze, 21, 59, 83, 107, 115, 159, 183, 207

    Apply, 8, 19, 22, 25, 35, 43, 46, 49, 59, 67, 73, 91, 94, 107, 119, 122, 125, 128, 135, 140, 146, 149, 159, 170, 176, 183, 197, 206, 207

    Brainstorm, 70

    Calculate, 41, 48, 63, 97

    Cite, 135

    Clarify, 11

    Classify, 15, 38, 39, 58, 68, 71, 90, 92, 116, 119, 126, 139, 142, 146, 166, 187

    Collaborate, 33, 57, 81, 105, 133, 157, 169, 181, 205

    Compare, 22, 42, 49, 73, 193, 199

    Create, 19, 52, 64, 76, 88, 91, 125, 134, 146, 173, 200

    Define, 147

    Discuss, 58

    Distinguish, 50

    Evaluate, 162

    Identify, 40, 44, 66, 121, 139, 141, 148, 150, 151, 165, 174

    Infer, 35, 124, 135, 198

    Interpret, 6, 17, 22, 23, 24, 43, 48, 63, 69, 71, 74, 87, 90, 93, 95, 98, 114, 118, 119, 120, 134, 147, 150, 163, 167, 168, 171, 189, 194, 197

    List, 143, 162

    Organize, 42

    Plan, 67, 96, 100, 164, 188, 189, 191, 194, 200

    Predict, 3, 10, 23, 34, 38, 47, 62, 64, 70, 82, 86, 92, 106, 117, 125, 139, 140, 144, 149, 182, 187, 194, 195, 196

    Prioritize, 82

    Rank, 72, 143, 158, 163, 186

    Sequence, 75, 76, 127, 174

    Solve, 172, 195

    Survey, 16, 88, 89, 138, 152

  Diagrams, 70, 73

  Grammar

    Comparative adjectives, 22, 42

    Count and noncount nouns, 67

    Future tense, 164, 188, 193

    How much and *How many,* 74

    Imperatives, 122, 176

    Infinitives, 140

    Information questions, 94

    Modals, 99, 149

    Negative imperatives, 76

    Past with *so,* 196

    Possessive adjectives, 8

    Prepositions, 97, 120

    Present continuous, 45

    Questions with *can,* 11, 64

    Simple past, 128, 145, 173

    Simple present, 16, 25, 40, 72, 118, 124, 141

    Some/any questions, 66

    Superlative adjectives, 22, 42

    these/those, 51

    this/that, 51

    Verbs

      be, 5, 16, 45, 68, 124, 145, 173

      have, 19, 72

      live, 16

      will, 164, 193

  Group activities, 5, 16, 40, 70, 91, 163, 176, 186

  Listening

    Classified ads, 169

    Conversations, 7, 10, 50, 52, 119, 144, 163

    Descriptions, 95

    Directions, 121

    Doctor's appointments, 145–146

    Educational choices, 190

    Emergencies, 151

    Food orders, 63

    Goals, 187, 192

    Greetings, 3–4

    Housing, 89, 92

    Instructions, 10–11, 76, 149, 174

    Job interviews, 171

    Numbers, 7

    Nutrition, 71

    Prices, 42

    Schedules, 23

  Matching

    Ailments, 154

    Goals, 194

    Instructions, 179

    Medical labels, 155

    Words and definitions, 98, 147, 172, 202

    Words and pictures, 89

  Partner activities, 4, 8, 9, 15, 21, 23, 25, 42, 66, 74, 94, 146, 164, 167, 170, 173, 190, 199

  Pronunciation

    Clarification words, 74

    Emphasis, 169

    /ez/ sound, 66

    /m/ sound, 4

    Rhythm, 69, 87

    this/these, 51

    Yes/No questions, 11, 15

    /z/ sound, 66

  Reading

    Advertisements, 47, 54

    Ailments, 142

    Budgets, 98

    Bus schedules, 115

    Calendars, 24

    Charts, 76, 143, 152, 189

    Classified ads, 91, 168

    Descriptions, 22

    Directions, 130

    Directories, 69

    Directory index, 118–119

    Emergencies, 150

    Envelopes, 126–127

    Evaluations, 162–163

    Family relationships, 17

    Flyers, 197

    Goals, 186

    Health, 139

    Housing, 87, 88, 95

    Job applications, 167, 170

    Job interviews, 171–172

    Maps, 120–122, 130

    Medical labels, 147–149

    Menus, 62–64, 78

    Messages and letters, 123–125, 131

    Receipts, 43, 48, 55

    Recipes, 74–76, 80

    Shopping lists, 70

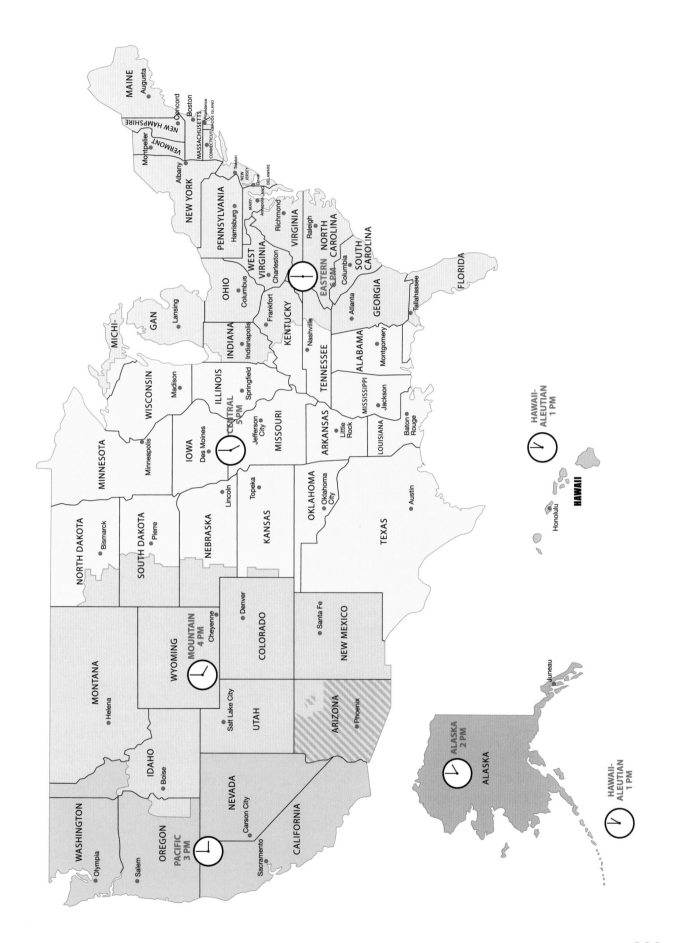